Successful Supervision

Successful Supervision

James R. H. White

Drawings by Bernard McCabe MSIA

McGRAW-HILL Book Company (UK) Limited

London · New York · St Louis · San Francisco · Auckland · Beirut
Bogotá · Düsseldorf · Johannesburg · Lisbon · Lucerne · Madrid
Mexico · Montreal · New Delhi · Panama · Paris · San Juan · São
Paulo · Singapore · Sydney · Tokyo · Toronto

Published by
McGraw-Hill Book Company (UK) Limited
MAIDENHEAD · BERKSHIRE · ENGLAND

Library of Congress Cataloging in Publication Data

White, James Richard Henry.
    Successful Supervision.

    Includes bibliographical references.
    1. Supervision of employees. 2. Personnel management.
    I. Title.
HF5549.W474   658.3   75-20066
ISBN 0-07-084458-5

45 678 HWV 81079

Printed and bound in Great Britain
by Hazell Watson & Viney Ltd, Aylesbury, Bucks

Contents

Preface   ix
Foreword: Your job and the law   xi
Note on action checklists   xii

1. *Achieving results through people*   1
    Employees' fears—how to foster the will to work—
    setting targets—how to build and motivate a team—
    communication and consultation—setting a good
    example

2. *Removing frustration, monotony, and nervous tension*   17
    How to beat frustration—make the job more
    interesting—cut down nervous tension

3. *Selecting staff*   25
    How to define what sort of person you are looking for
    —job specification and man specification—how to
    prepare for the interview—asking the right questions
    in an interview—obtaining truthful references

4. *Introducing the new employee*   39
    How to reduce staff turnover through good
    induction—what the new person needs to know—
    what you need to know about him—following
    through on induction

5. *Your responsibility for training*   47
    How to develop your own ability—what to read—
    taking advantage of opportunities—identifying the
    training you need—how to train your subordinate
    supervisors—delegation, deputizing, project work,
    committee assignments, guided experience, job
    rotation—how to train non-supervisory staff—why
    some supervisors fail in this—helping people to learn
    —successful job instruction—how to make individual
    and section training plans

6. *Understanding complaints and grievances*   70
    The difference between a complaint and a grievance
    —grievances in disguise—five good tips for grievance
    interviews—know your company's grievance
    procedure

7. *Introducing changes*   78
    Why your people may resist changes—how you can
    win them over—telling them in advance and
    consulting them about the new arrangements

8. *Reducing disciplinary problems*   86
    How to create the right environment—setting an
    example—knowing your ground—how to put
    somebody on the right lines without arousing
    resentment—the two-stage interview—know your
    company's disciplinary procedure

9. *Your responsibility for communication*   98
    Dinosaur Ltd—the need to relay information both
    ways—how to communicate with your staff—and
    with your boss—what each needs to know

10. *The supervisor's responsibility for safety*   106
    How to promote safety—your legal responsibility—
    older employees—youngsters—the accident prone

11. *Your shop steward and you*   131
What unions are for—the shop steward's job—how
to work effectively with him—the need for courtesy—
his role when you reprimand an employee—know the
law, the union and the procedures—don't delegate
supervisory jobs to him

12. *Don't do it all yourself*   140
Getting others to do the work—letting them make
decisions—you carry the can—thirteen steps to
better delegation

13. *The organization you work in*   150
The different parts of an organization—the role of
directors, managers, supervisors and operatives—line
organization—functional supervision—line and staff
—authority and responsibility—how to recognize
organizational problems which could be making
things difficult for you

14. *What you can do to improve work methods*   161
The six steps of method improvement. The
questioning technique

15. *Cost reduction*   166
Cost reduction for all supervision—what is meant by
productivity—the need to cut costs—six ideas
for improving productivity—value analysis
Cost reduction for factory production supervisors—
machine paced jobs with slack—down time—make sure
men report waiting time—cutting down on unnecessary
work and rework—how to get standards right
Some useful cost accounting terns to know—labour
costs—direct and indirect—material costs—variable
and fixed overheads—standard costing procedures—quiz
on cost terms

16. *Some special aspects of supervision* 184
Your deputy—women employees—their motivation
—the law as it affects them—the older employee—
what he can and can't do—helping an employee to
prepare for retirement

17. *Planning and managing your time* 193
You must make time to plan—how to work out
systems for recurring jobs—year to view organizers—
checklists—schedules of jobs—finding your best
working time—planning a big job—job breakdowns
—developing the right habits—the rush job

18. *Using initiative when work is delegated to you* 209
Completed staff work—preventive and contingency
plans—creative thinking

19. *Management tool subjects* 214
26 management terms explained

20. *Employee appraisals* 221
Why appraise staff?—the employee's needs—how to
set standards—what kinds of measurement to use—
checklist for staff about to be appraised—how to
prepare for and conduct a job review interview—a
four point plan—the art of listening—asking the
right questions—reflecting

21. *Supervision in the office* 232
The need to liaise with other departments—breaking
down lateral communication barriers—self development for office supervisors—training staff—further
education—improving office efficiency—teamwork
and group behaviour

Index 241

Preface

The duties of a supervisor will depend to a great extent on the kind of business he is in, but basically what he needs to know can be put under two headings: *technical aspects* and *supervision*. This book deals exclusively with supervision.

It is designed to help section and department heads, whether they are controlling production processes, construction projects, service units, or clerical work, to manage their jobs more effectively and be better team leaders. I have used the masculine gender for convenience, but the book applies equally to both sexes.

Managers, training directors and tutors will also find it extremely useful as a textbook to be used in conjunction with other methods of supervisory training. Staff who are intending to take examinations leading to the NEBSS Certificate or the Institute of Supervisory Management's Certificate in Supervisory Studies should be encouraged to answer the questions at the end of the chapters. Office supervisors should read chapter 21 first so that they can see the rest of the book in perspective.

The ideas contained here owe much to the 20 000 supervisors, managers and directors from industry, commerce and local government who have discussed their jobs with me, especially my friends and former colleagues from Shell International and The Industrial Society. Mr Laurie Sapper, LLB, General Secretary of the Association of University Teachers, has provided valuable advice on the legal aspects of employment.

I am grateful to Mr Bernard McCabe, MSIA, for illustrating the book so well, and conveying the exact message with his excellent cartoons.

Finally I wish to thank Mrs Gillian Grenfell for her co-operation in producing this book.

Foreword: Your job and the law

In the last few years there has been a marked increase in the number of laws governing the employment of staff, and this trend looks like continuing. Books on industrial relations law seem to be out of date before they come off the press these days, so I shall not describe the current position here, but you have to be alert to the legal implications of what you do as head of your section or department.

The following general principles are unlikely to change:

1. When staff are recruited they are entitled to receive certain information about their terms and conditions of employment.
2. During the period of their employment the law affords some protection against unreasonable working conditions, industrial disease and accidents.
3. Dismissals have to be handled carefully according to certain legal requirements which are based on the concept that a man's job is a possession which must not be taken away from him unless he is seriously at fault, and if this should happen, he is entitled to some compensation for the loss of it.

So if you have to engage staff, make anyone redundant, discipline them, or dismiss for misconduct you must bear this in mind, as well as the provisions relating to safety, injury, health and welfare. As you know, special rules apply to the employment and remuneration of women.

If you are ever in doubt about the current position on this or any other point of law and your company does not employ a personnel officer, suggest to your manager that you should seek the advice of the Department of Employment. Their industrial relations advisory staff are most helpful and, besides giving advice, they will recommend to you, or provide, the most up-to-date explanatory booklets on the point in question.

Keep your eyes open for announcements in the press concerning new legislation and ask your personnel department (or whoever does that job) for the latest booklets which might have a bearing on industrial relations in your department.

Note on action checklists

This book is called *Successful Supervision* because it is designed to help you regularly examine your own strong points and see where you could do better.

Ask your manager to go through some of the checklists with you, giving a tick where you both think you are O K and a cross where attention is needed. This will give you a clearer understanding of your priorities and targets for improvement. If he considers that an important and sometimes overlooked point should be added to the checklist, be sure to include that in your action plan as well.

Ask him a few months later how he feels you have been doing. Some managers are too busy, or just too cautious to give you this vital information unless you ask for it.

1. *Achieving results through people*

Every supervisor achieves his results through other people and the measure of his effectiveness is the extent to which he develops and directs their combined creative powers. Staff must first be selected wisely according to the kind of work for which they are needed, and then trained to do it well. The techniques of selection and training which are explained in later chapters will help you if your company expects you to play a part in this process.

When your staff have been recruited and started their training, how do you encourage them to give of their best to their work? The first essential is to identify the reasons why people deliberately restrict their output, and find ways of removing these causes. Once this is done, it is important to see how, in a group which has no reason not to work, a positive creative drive can be fostered.

Why do people restrict their output?

Apart from go-slow and work-to-rule orders being used against management openly to force their hand, there are three main reasons why people restrict their output. They all stem from insecurity, and their remedy is only partially in your hands. When you see them operating you should first do what you can within the limits of your authority to remove them, and then advise senior management on any further remedial action you suggest might be taken.

Fear of running short of work

Staff like to see that there is plenty of work coming along to keep them busy during the day. This keeps up their piecework earnings, if they are paid in that way, and protects their over-time.

You can remove this fear temporarily by reassuring them about the forward order position, but sooner or later a bad patch is bound to come along. The only effective way in which the fear can ultimately be removed is by guaranteeing them a good wage. This means two things: first, either no piecework or a small variable piecework margin over and above a good basic wage; and second, the overtime habit must not be allowed to develop.

Fear that the piecerate may be cut

Piecerates, whether time-studied or arrived at by guesswork, tend to slacken when people find short cuts. But instead of the company and the operator benefiting from the latter's increased experience, neither does, because the operator is careful not to work to capacity in case the rates are revised.

Improved rate-setting is partly the answer, but it is also necessary to guarantee staff that rates will not be revised unless there is a change of method. Still, the problem persists, in that wages will become inflated unless output is restricted, and when the next job comes along to be time-studied, pay packets will suffer. Many companies, like Corah's of Leicester (see page 5) are wondering whether piecerates do not, in many cases, reduce output rather than increase it. I think that in a shop where piecework payment has been used for many years, the output is often the same as it would be if men worked at their natural pace, because the checks and balances will have operated over the years to remove the short-term stimulus of payment by results.

Fear of redundancy

Five people will hold back from doing the work of six if it means that the sixth will be made redundant. So it is important that you should try to plan your manpower requirements in advance. The firm may have to carry redundant staff for short periods pending vacancies arising elsewhere in the organization rather than sack staff and then a few weeks later have to recruit more. A few companies have introduced various forms of guaranteed employment for life. Others have improved their redundancy payments. All these measures help, in varying degrees, to eliminate restrictive practices which have been adopted through the fear of redundancy.

How to foster the will to work

So far I have talked about trying to remove the deterrents which make people hold back their full potential. Once this has been done, how do we elicit active and enthusiastic effort?

The key to this is to ask yourself what you as an employee want from your job. The list will probably include these items:

▷ a good salary,
▷ security,
▷ job satisfaction (see good results without too much frustration),
▷ an interesting job,
▷ a challenge,
▷ a good team spirit, cooperation,
▷ dignity—respect from fellow employees and fellow citizens,
▷ comfortable and safe working conditions,
▷ being kept in the picture,
▷ a chance to use your brains and talents,
▷ a hearing for your complaints,
▷ reasonable leisure,
▷ the opportunity to learn and progress.

People's priorities vary, of course, according to their age, sex, family commitments, experience and personality, so if you know your staff as individuals you can strike the right note with each one. For example, you will not persuade a 16-year-old girl to take a job by praising the firm's pension scheme—but status, team spirit and reasonable leisure will almost certainly attract her.

A skilful supervisor can anticipate and avoid a grievance by spotting where a person's needs are not being satisfied in his work, and sometimes either move him or change the content of his job. The industrial psychologist Herzberg points out that removing dissatisfaction in this way is an important step *towards* motivating people, but it will not in itself make people work with greater enthusiasm. To do this you have to give them the opportunity to achieve something—either as individuals or, better still, as members of a team—because this will make them want to win the approval of their colleagues.

Give people something to aim for

We all do a better job when we are given an aim. This target should be a reasonably challenging, but not impossible one, and we need to see how well we are doing at every stage of

Give people something to aim for

progress towards it. One of the most important developments in management thinking during the past 25 years has been the technique known as Management by Objectives (MbO). Production managers, sales directors, accountants—the whole management team—are encouraged to put down on paper, with the guidance of their superior, the main activities which the company requires them to carry out. Then in each activity they set one or two targets which will contribute to the firm's specified objectives.

The same psychology can be applied at all levels. The supervisor's targets are the completion of production batches, the meeting of delivery deadlines, completing maintenance schedules, and so on. The clerks, operators, craftsmen and technicians, whose efforts achieve these results, need to see their own goals clearly, and feel they are making progress towards them. In many cases people's results vary in direct proportion to management's interest in their performance.

The well known Leicester textile firm of Corah Ltd have moved away from piecework in favour of monthly progress discussions. Each operative is interviewed by her manager at the end of every month. He discusses her performance, tells her whether or not she is to be promoted to a higher grade, or encourages her to improve if her targets are not met. This personal interest in the girl's performance puts the emphasis on producing the right quality of garment in the required quantities. There have been steady improvements in departmental productivity, increased flexibility, and, above all, a new attitude stemming from the security of a guaranteed wage.

Show appreciation

We all like to have someone take an interest in what we are doing and how we are getting on with the job. Some people think that to show appreciation is unnecessary. You know the way it goes:

WIFE: Did you like your dinner?
HUSBAND (*from behind newspaper*): My what, dear? . . . dinner?
         Oh, all right.

Most of us would rather have constructive criticism than complete indifference, but criticism, too, can be a cumulative poison. Sincere appreciation works best. These days people do not often have responsibility for a complete job—like, say, making a piece of furniture, or forging a horseshoe. The masterpiece of which you could say 'all my own work' used itself to confer on its maker a mark of appreciation and encouragement. But today, when nobody has the full responsibility for the job, nobody gets the complete satisfaction of finishing it. The supervisor can make up for this deficiency by being sincerely appreciative.

Help to build a team

It is important to understand something about the psychology of group behaviour so that you can build a team. Many of our most profound needs are met by belonging to a group. We suffer without team support, or if we are forced into groups which do not share our values. Groups have great power over their members, and people will sacrifice money, or sometimes the approval of society as a whole, if they have to choose between these and acceptance by their fellows.

A group, of whatever kind—sports club, gang, social clique, or working team—has three main functions:

▷ to do something in common;
▷ to maintain itself (it has a will to survive);
▷ to satisfy the needs of its members.

As a supervisor you can make use of these forces among your own staff in the following ways:

Emphasize the common interest shared by them and the company. Make WORK the group's objective

Ensure that everybody knows how important their product or service is, and what their section's goals are. You have to show real enthusiasm if you expect them to be keen. When you present a group of people with a challenging and worthwhile aim, it is easier to motivate them and keep them on the correct path. A good example of this is the story of Leicester's Kamakazi motorcyclists.

Police Constable Tidmarsh of Leicester (who confesses to being motorbike mad himself) had so often booked the various members of a group of high spirited young enthusiasts whose motorcycles could present something of a problem on the city's roads, that it was becoming a meaningless routine. Yet there must be, he thought, a better way of dealing with the problem than just escalating the punishments given.

So he called together the ringleaders ('in a room with the one

Kamakazi

light bulb padlocked in'), got to know them and their code of conduct, and became aware that buried just below the surface was a 'knights of the road' outlook. The idea was developed in discussions with them. They would help road users who were in difficulties, and present displays at fairs, fetes and rallies. The proceeds would be ploughed back into a self-financing club, and they could make a considerable contribution to charity by being the main attraction at these events.

Soon the pipe dream became a reality, and under the name of the Kamakazi Motor Cycle Rodeo they enjoy a reputation second to none for putting on spectacular displays. These include driving through blazing tunnels of straw bales, and motorcycle leaps from a ramp, one of which is included in the *Guinness Book of Records*. In their third year of operation they presented 24 shows and made £1500 towards the maintenance of the 30 machines they now own. Their code of conduct matches their prowess and includes such unwritten rules as 'Don't get into trouble with the law', and 'Don't do the show for personal gain'.

All PC Tidmarsh did was to help the group find a new outlet and a more useful set of goals, while being careful to preserve it as a team and look after the needs of individual members (see below). It helps if, like Mr Tidmarsh, you yourself are enthusiastic about the subject. (If you want a good motorcycle rodeo now you know where to get one.)

Look after the group

Understand the needs of the group, safeguard the standards which they consider important, and look after them in ways which they think important.

Plan the work so that members have to depend on each other, and so that the value of each individual's work is clear to the group. This will strengthen loyalties. It is a mistake to try and play one person off against another and rule by division. Any enthusiasm people may have for the job soon dissolves each morning with the prospect of having to work in an unfriendly atmosphere. If you can foster goodwill among staff you will find that they develop a sense of responsibility for the whole section's good, and if one member makes a mistake or is temporarily absent they will put in extra effort to compensate.

A group cannot survive without good communication, so keep them informed about the department's progress, and about each other's work. Explain and discuss orders, and *consult*.

Look after the members

Study and look after the people in the group, not just their work. Each person should see his job as difficult, but important. Try to organize the jobs so that they present an element of challenge.

See that they have the right tools

Good tools enable the work to be done better, more quickly and with the most economical use of skilled manpower. They show the staff that management is concerned for the quality of the job and that the person who has to do it matters.

A well-known brand of typewriter used to be advertised on

London tube trains with the heading. 'The . . . on your desk shows you that he cares'. The idea behind it was to bully the poor executive into thinking that if his own secretary saw the advertisement she would leave him and move to somewhere where an 'X' typewriter had been provided. Perhaps people won't go to those extremes, but good tools and equipment do help to attract and keep good employees, besides enabling people to realize their full productive potential. Nobody wants to work twice as hard as he needs in order to make up for the deficiencies of his equipment or the environment in which he is expected to use it.

Give staff credit for brains as well as brawn

If the work permits, let people use their own discretion on some of the decisions to be made. This makes the job more interesting and staff will work more conscientiously if they feel they are implementing their own ideas and so proving their own judgement.

Consult

Besides letting them use their own judgement on how to do a particular job, make a practice of consulting on wider issues. Because you ask a man's opinion on a matter which affects him or his work, it doesn't follow that you have to be bound by it. You don't have to abide by a majority decision. You are the one who is paid to make the decisions, so if, after weighing up all the pros and cons, you decide that you have to go against a subordinate's advice, you must do so.

Listen to suggestions

Some companies introduce suggestion schemes because they know that those closest to the job have a great many useful ideas which could cut costs, improve the product, avoid waste, or make the process easier. Whether or not your company runs a suggestion scheme, show an interest in your employees' ideas and see that they are given a fair trial. Make sure that if they are not workable the originator is told why, and see that he gets the credit for an idea that *does* work. Money is the most tangible reward for good ideas, but many progressive firms consider they pay a man to use his brains as well as his muscles, and that ultimately his inventiveness will win him promotion. There obviously should be *some* reward, if not an immediate financial one.

See that they are fairly paid

Groucho Marx said 'Money may not be able to buy happiness, but you can make a substantial down payment with it.' Most people, of course, do work mainly for money, and if you consider that any member of your staff is not being paid fairly it is up to you to try to get something done about it. You do not have to let him know that you think he is not getting what he is worth, and most probably you will not have the final word on whether or not he is given a rise. But you should get all the facts—what he is paid, and why you think he deserves more—and tell your superior what you recommend.

A person's *wage* should match his *ability*, and his ability should match the *job*. If one of these three elements is out of line with the other two, whether higher or lower, you can expect trouble.

Fig. 1.1

wage	ability	job	√
wage			
	ability	job	×
	ability		
wage		job	×
		job	
wage	ability		×

Some supervisors take the view: 'Why should I bother? I shall only get myself a bad name for being a nuisance. If he isn't satisfied he can take it up with the union and let them have a go at management—they'll sort it out.' This kind of attitude builds up distrust between management and the staff, fosters the feeling that to obtain justice you have to fight the company, makes nonsense of all efforts to build a sense of common purpose, and in the long run is of great disservice to the organization.

It is not the union's prerogative to manage, and it does not usually want to. But in some firms it has begun to do so because management has abdicated its responsibility to its employees. Staff think that 'everything we have, the union has won for us'.

Set a good example

People in your section will take their cue from your behaviour and attitude to the job. Your punctuality, neatness, high standards and safety-mindedness, speak louder than words and will achieve a great deal more as far as the staff are concerned.

Require high standards

Do not tolerate poor work. The customer has a right to expect a good quality product and will take his business elsewhere if he doesn't get it. Staff like to take a pride in what they do, and they know that their security depends on the quality of the goods they are turning out.

Tell people the reasons for doing a job

When people know the purpose of a job and why it is wanted by tomorrow, or why it is to be of a special quality, they put extra effort into it. Knowing what it is for, they can use their own initiative to make decisions concerning it, such as whether to use a certain finish or what improvization they could make for the sake of speed. 'Theirs is not to reason why' went out with the Charge of the Light Brigade. Once the rush job is finished, make sure it is taken away out of sight even if the urgency has for some reason abated. It is pretty frustrating for those who put themselves out to complete it, to see that the urgency was all a false alarm.

Help to create and maintain pride in the company

Borden (UK) Limited produce food-packaging films and a wide range of synthetic resins and adhesives, particularly for industrial purposes. Their uses range from furniture manufacture to sand-bonding applications in the foundry industry. The company sees to it that the uses to which their products are put are known on the shopfloor. Whereas in the old days it might have been known as 'the glue factory' it now has a very different image.

Whatever your product is, you probably feel enthusiastic about it, so convey your keenness to others. People like to work for a firm whose name is a household word and associated with quality. If you play your part in helping to foster a pride in the company, speak well of it, adopt a constructive attitude, and play your part in building up good public relations, you will be helping to mould the company image. If all the supervisors and managers in the company do this it will quickly earn the reputation of being a good firm to work for.

These, in fact, are the guidelines most frequently mentioned by managers and supervisors in discussions on the subject of winning the staff's cooperation. They are all based on the obvious but often forgotten fact that we all work better if we are given a worthwhile job to do, and feel that we are being treated like responsible people while we get on with it.

Fig. 1.2. Checklist on leadership

Questions	× √	Notes
1. Do you take positive steps to do what you can to remove the causes of any deliberate restriction of output?		
2. Do you give people objectives or targets, and show interest in and appreciation of their progress towards them?		
3. Do you show sincere appreciation of people's work?		
4. Do you consciously try to build their self-confidence?		
5. Do you give them the reasons for special jobs?		
6. Do you help to create and maintain pride in the company?		
7. Do you try to build a team?		
8. Do you expect high standards of performance?		
9. Do you give your staff credit for brains as well as brawn?		
10. Do you consult them, and keep them involved?		
11. Do you listen to their suggestions?		

Questions	× √	Notes
12. If a suggestion is unworkable, do you explain to the originator the reason why?		
13. Do you try to see that they are fairly paid?		
14. Do you give them the equipment and facilities they need to do the job?		
15. Do you set a good example in: ▷ timekeeping? ▷ attitude to the job? ▷ attitude to the company? ▷ tidiness? ▷ safety?		
16. Do you know each member of your staff— his background, hobbies, education, training, experience, and personality?		
17. Do you listen to their problems when they want you to?		
18. Do you show a contagious enthusiasm?		
19. Do you have daily contact with each member of staff?		
20. Do you back up your staff when they need your support?		
21. Do you allocate the right job to the right person, using everybody's talents to the full?		
22. Do you foster pride in the job?		
23. Do you allocate to each person a special area of expertise and responsibility?		
24. Do you take positive steps to increase job interest?		
25. Do you plan the work carefully to avoid unnecessary effort and to keep them busy?		
26. Do you lead by example?		
27. Do you put pace-setters in with each work group?		

Questions	X √	Notes
28. Do you try to improve their working conditions, hygiene and safety?		
29. Are you careful about the selection and training of subordinate supervisors?		
30. Do you interview people who resign, retire, etc., from your department in order to find out good and bad points about the job and the environment?		

Questions

1. It is claimed that a substantial improvement in productivity could be achieved by encouraging the development of team spirit. Discuss this claim, and show how such a spirit could be developed within an organization.

2. Do you think it is possible to develop powers of leadership? If so, why? If not, why not?

2. Removing frustration, monotony and nervous tension

People often put more into the job than the results seem to show. Their efforts go to waste on *frustration*, *monotony*, and *nervous tension*. Spoiled work and abortive effort are sometimes caused by domestic trouble which you cannot do much about, but you may be able to eliminate some or all of the first three items.

Frustration

Work that you feel is being done needlessly or fruitlessly always requires more effort and leaves you unsatisfied at the end of the day.

Good planning and organizing will avoid unnecessary hold-ups, and it is important to plan sufficiently in advance of the job so that once it is under way staff do not have to be switched from one project to another. If your kind of work requires this type of flexibility, make sure that when you select staff you choose people whose attitude of mind and previous experience fit them for it. Adequate explanations of the need to switch priorities, and plenty of chance for staff to let off steam when you do, will reduce their irritation. Unless there's an emergency, ask your staff to fit new jobs in when they can.

Frustration is sometimes caused by delegating duties which are beyond the ability, experience, or terms of reference of the employee. Make sure that the employee has the necessary qualifications and sufficient authority to see the job through.

When your staff are frustrated by the system within which they work, the actions or inertia of another department, inefficient lines of communication, or red tape, show them what you can do for them by taking up their case and seeing it through to as satisfactory a conclusion as possible.

Make sure that you see every member of your staff each day —or at least twice a week. Daily contact ensures that you become aware of their problems as they arise, and can take early action where necessary. By simply being on hand you will cut their frustration by half.

Some frustration arises from a thwarted desire to progress to a better, more interesting job. It pays to win for your department a reputation as a stepping stone to better things, so give your staff the opportunity to progress. Put forward the names of your most suitable people when top management is head hunting for the next generation of managers. You should be counting your management output—how many supervisors are you developing? How many managers will look back on their first opportunity and have you to thank for it?

If you respect your staff for the jobs they are performing at their present level in the company, and see to it that their conditions and job titles are ones they can accept with self respect, one possible source of frustration at least will be removed.

Monotony

N. V. Philips' Gloeilampenfabrieken, the international electrical and electronics company, has for 14 years been developing the concept of *work structuring* (or *job enrichment*) and in many cases it has obtained significant increases in productivity. The idea is to rearrange work so that it will be fit for human beings to perform, instead of organizing the job in accordance with the needs of technology and forcing people to fit in with its demands. They define work structuring: 'The organization of work, the work situation and the work circumstances are structured in such a way that, while maintaining or improving efficiency, job content accords as closely as possible with the capabilities and ambitions of the individual employee: . . . a total integration of technical, economic and social aims.'

The late Douglas McGregor pointed out in 1960 (*The Human Side of Enterprise*, McGraw-Hill) that under modern conditions of industrial life few people are given the chance to use their brains. He distinguished two sets of beliefs about attitudes to work, Theory X and Theory Y. According to Theory Y:

1. Work is as natural to most people as play or rest, and people are not basically lazy. Under the right conditions they can enjoy working.
2. Punishment is not the only way of getting them to do the job. They will discipline themselves if they really believe in what the company is trying to do.
3. People will be keen on their work if it is satisfying to them. They will find it so if it gives them a sense of importance, and the chance to use their abilities.
4. Under the right conditions most will look for responsibility. When they avoid it, have no ambition, and look only for security, you usually find that this attitude stems from the way they have been treated in the past.
5. Those with imagination, ingenuity, and creative talents are not few and far between. Most of the population have these qualities, and every company could make fuller use of its employees' talents in order to guarantee its success and security.

Theory X, on the other hand assumes that:

1. The average human being dislikes work and will avoid it if he can.
2. Therefore most people have to be forced, threatened, closely supervised and made to get on with the job.
3. Most people prefer to be directed, wish to avoid responsibility, have little ambition, and only want security.

Theory Y questions some of the approaches suggested by work study. Perhaps the scientific solution to a production

Removing frustration, monotony and nervous tension **19**

problem is not always the most effective unless it fully takes into account the human element.

Some of the Philips' research findings seem to show that in a minority of cases certain groups of teenage girls are less likely to respond to Theory Y than those who look on their work as a long-term career, and in these cases they want physical comfort,

People are doing jobs which machines could do

pleasant conditions, and good wages. Monotony does not matter—it leaves the mind free to think of more important prospects. I think that they are a minority of the working population, but it shows that the supervisor must know his own people and their needs. Although he is not in a position to reorganize working methods except on a small scale and subject to approval from superiors and colleagues, he is likely to achieve better results if he treats people in a way which reflects a belief in Theory Y.

Efficiency can be boosted by encouraging training. This helps even manual workers in jobs where there is only slight opportunity for promotion. In gangs of railway labourers, a few of the supervisors taught the men some facts over and above the details which were strictly necessary. The following figures show that, because it taught them more than the absolute essentials of their present jobs, this training boosted job interest and productivity:

	Percentage of men who said that their supervisor taught them new duties
High-producing gangs	39
Low-producing gangs	19

You can further reduce monotony by showing your interest in a job. The cleaner will put more thought and enthusiasm into dusting the desk and bench tops down if you discuss how important it is to do it well, and what could be done to make the job easier or more effective. Involvement in decision making and discussions with you about the way jobs are done will make the employee see himself as an important part of the team.

Where possible, give people extra responsibility. If someone has to fetch and carry a ladder, make him responsible for checking on its condition and reporting any deterioration. Let him be the guardian of the key and the padlock which secures it after use. If someone has to use stationery, make her responsible for maintaining minimum stock levels, and if possible reordering where necessary.

If you can delegate responsibility according to the particular talents and standards of an employee—such as giving to the ex-fire-station labourer the responsibility for cleaning the brass-work—you will thus be recognizing him as an individual and he will relish the job (provided that wasn't his reason for leaving the fire brigade).

Your own enthusiasm for the work of the team as a whole will rub off on the members even though they do not go around openly professing it. By being enthusiastic you can stir up interest in even the most monotonous job. Figure 2.1 gives some guidelines for enriching the content of jobs. You can no doubt adopt some of these ideas in your own department:

Fig. 2.1

Principle	*Motivators involved*
1. Remove some controls, but retain accountability.	Responsibility and personal achievement.

> *Example:* the cleaner draws her own polishes, etc., straight from the store, but has a monthly budget.

2. Increase the accountability of individuals for their own work.	Responsibility and recognition.

> *Example:* the clerk in the pay office has to account to the worker if she has made a mistake. No office supervisor shields her.

3. Give a person a complete natural unit of work (module, division, area, etc.).	Responsibility, achievement and recognition.

> *Example:* a service engineer has his own area.

4. Grant additional authority to an employee in his activity; promote job freedom.	Responsibility, achievement and recognition.

> *Example:* flexible working hours.

5. Make periodic reports directly available to the worker himself rather than to the supervisor.	Internal recognition.

> *Example:* a weaver gets his own loom efficiency % figures daily.

Principle	Motivators involved
6. Introduce new and more difficult tasks not previously dealt with.	Growth and learning.

Example: operating a more complex machine.

Principle	Motivators involved
7. Assign individuals specific or specialized tasks, enabling them to become experts.	Responsibility, growth and advancement.

Example: an electrical engineer shows interest in electronic gadgetry and takes charge of research and development in automation.

Nervous tension

Nervous tension can develop from unreasonably demanding workloads or from bosses who induce a sense of failure in order to spur people on.

A group of girls in a dressmaking factory were given an impossible target of 180 dozen garments a day on the assumption that if they aimed at that figure they would not fall far short of it. The work study department knew from their calculations that 140 dozen was about the limit, but the girls were not aware of this. When they saw how poorly they seemed to be getting along, their output dropped to under 100 dozen.

A psychologist who was advising management suggested that a few girls should be told the real quota but asked to keep it secret for the purpose of the experiment. When this was done, the output of those who were in the know increased at once to 120.

A similar experiment was performed on some students whose muscular tension was electrically measured while they were doing light work. Half of them were told that they were doing it poorly while the others were praised and given every encouragement. It was found that the 'failure' group were 25% more tense than the 'success' group while working and twice as tense immediately after they had finished the job. Not only had they put more into it but they were not able to relax so well afterwards.

At times every job produces monotony, frustration and nervous tension and we shall never eliminate these completely. But we can reduce their frequency if we recognize the symptoms when staff show signs of strain, consult them on ways of reducing tension and boredom, and take all possible steps to stop this waste of energy.

Solvitur ambulando

Worry, frustration and tension can be reduced if you maintain the sense of progress in your team. The motto 'solvitur ambulando' means that problems are often solved by moving forward instead of worrying about an existing situation. You stay afloat by moving forwards. It is what the business is becoming rather than what it is today which is important, and its managers will be accepted as leaders only if their staff can see that they are going somewhere.

Things live by moving and gain strength as they go (*Virgil*).

Questions

1. What are the main factors which create nervous tension at work, and how can they be reduced?

2. How might a company improve the job satisfaction of its employees?

3. Selecting staff

A company once decided to buy a machine worth £10 000. There was a careful analysis of its capacity, potential and durability. All those who were going to install it, use it, service it, and pay for it, had a lengthy conference and at last after all these deliberations, it was bought and carefully installed. A machine had been selected.

It is ironical that so often a new employee who will spend twenty years with the company and cost in wages and overheads over £50 000 in that time, is selected in ten minutes.

How do you select a person for a job?

There are three stages to go through:

1. Write a *job specification*. (What does the person have to *do* in this job?)
2. Write a *man specification*. (What does the ideal candidate have to *be*?)
3. Conduct the *interview*.

You must define the job before you can move on to stage 2 and say what sort of person you will need in order to fill it. When you come to stage 2, the man specification, consider the items shown on the left-hand side of the form (Fig. 3.2): physical, attainments, intelligence, special aptitudes, interests, disposition, circumstances, and age. The following notes will guide your thoughts when doing this.

Duties and responsibilities

Main routine duties.
Special responsibilities for other people, equipment or material.
Commonest difficulties among duties or responsibilities.

Working conditions and rewards

Nature of workplace (damp, dirty, noisy, etc.).
Nature of work (heavy, dirty, unvaried, solitary, etc.).
Social opportunities of work (companionship, prestige, team-work, etc.).
What do workers say they like *most* about the work?
What do workers say they like *least* about it?
Anything else to be noted?

Personal characteristics

Physical. Is it important that he should be free of any defects of health or physique that may be of occupational importance? Is his appearance, bearing or speech important?

Attainments (educational or occupational). What type of education should he have had? How well should he have done educationally? What occupational training and experience should he have had already? How well should he have done occupationally?

General intelligence (upper and lower limits). How much general intelligence should he display?

Specialized aptitudes (verbal, manual, mechanical, etc.). Must he have any marked mechanical aptitude? Manual dexterity? Facility in the use of words or figures? Talent for drawing or music?

Interests. Would it be useful if he showed intellectual, practical, constructional, physically active, social or artistic interests?

Disposition. Should he be more acceptable, more influential, more dependable, more self-reliant than most?

Circumstances. What should be his domestic circumstances? (Commitments, general background, relationships if important.)

Availability. Can he start when you want him to?

Figures 3.1 and 3.2 show blank forms for stages 1 and 2 and Figs 3.3 and 3.4 show them when completed (a storekeeper's job is used as an example).

Fig. 3.1. Job specification form

Job title :

Duties :

Responsible to :

Supervises :

Other relationships :

    Internal :

    External :

Fig. 3.2. Man specification form

Must	Should
PHYSICAL	
ATTAINMENTS	
INTELLIGENCE	
SPECIAL APTITUDES	
INTERESTS	
DISPOSITION	
CIRCUMSTANCES	
AGE	

Fig. 3.3. Completed job specification form for storekeeper

Job title :	Storekeeper.
Duties :	Supervise stores staff.
	Issue stores items against departmental orders.
	Maintain stock levels, reordering when necessary.
	Stock taking.
	Keep records of stock usage.
	Local purchase.
	Return defective equipment and materials to suppliers.
	Keep store tidy.
	Operate fork lift truck when required.
Responsible to :	Factory superintendent.
Supervises :	2 storemen, 2 labourers.
Other relationships :	
Internal :	Staff from all departments.
External :	Suppliers. Contractors.

Fig. 3.4. Completed man specification form for storekeeper

Must	Should

PHYSICAL
   Good health.
   Good hearing.
   Not below average
   physical strength.	

ATTAINMENTS
   Some previous store
   keeping experience.
   Good primary education.
	Storekeeping experience in this industry.
	Some experience of successful supervision

INTELLIGENCE Average commonsense.	

SPECIAL APTITUDES
   Good at simple arithmetic.
   Clear handwriting.
   Orderly way of working.	

INTERESTS	Mechanical and practical.

DISPOSITION
   Helpful and cooperative
   attitude.
   Tactful in supervising his
   staff.
   Honest.	

CIRCUMSTANCES
   No home circumstances
   requiring much time off.
	Not live too far from factory so that he will not be delayed by bad weather, etc.
	Married (or other stabilizing influence).

AGE 21–55	24–45

After completion of stages 1 and 2, you will be ready for stage 3, which is the interview.

Conducting the interview

Preparation

Look at the application form before you see the candidate. These forms enable you to sort out the non-starters, and you can save everybody's time by saying something like 'Thank you for filling in the form. This job is not cut out for you as it doesn't fit your qualifications. Perhaps we could keep your name on record for one which does?'

If you receive too many unsuitable applicants this means that your advertisement should be more specific about the qualifications needed. By being as detailed as you can in setting out your requirements, you will save people's time and trouble.

If the completed application form looks promising, mark your man specification accordingly. Make a note on the application form so that you can fill in any missing information at the interview, and perhaps identify useful leads which would open up the topics you wish to discuss. For example, 'number of children' is a useful lead into the subject of domestic circumstances if these are relevant.

Notice any unexplained gaps in employment. Has he changed jobs too frequently? Five job changes in 15 years is usually about the limit. What can you learn from the way the form is filled in, about such aspects as intelligence, literacy, neatness?

Find somewhere private for the interview, and try to ensure comfort and freedom from interruptions.

The interview

You want to know all about the applicant so he should do nearly all the talking. Put him at ease and prepare an opening remark to break the ice. From his application form perhaps you can find something you have in common. When you have explained the job, its benefits, and told him the salary, start him talking. Work all subjects round to cover the questions you need answered.

Applicants are often reticent in interviews. Occasionally you will come across the loafer who does not want the job anyway, and will go away happily if you write 'unsuitable' on the paper he was given by the Department of Employment. Spot him early on and politely show him the door.

Assuming that he wants the job but is tonguetied, try to get him onto a topic that he feels strongly about. A gliding analogy illustrates this point: a glider pilot will attempt to get his aircraft into a 'thermal' of rising warm air which carries him up and then gives him momentum for a long flight. Hitting on a point which matters to an interviewee is a bit like this. He warms to his theme, and gives you some interesting leads. You can spot the 'thermals' because he uses words which convey feelings such as pride, determination, regret, indignation, etc. Sometimes the intonation of the voice reveals a particular feeling, like surprise, enthusiasm, anger, or sorrow.

An interview might go like this:

APPLICANT (*for garage supervisor's job*): I heard about the job from one of the other parents at the PTA.
INTERVIEWER: PTA?
APPLICANT: Yes, the parent/teachers association at the school. I usually go along there and put a word in once a month.
INTERVIEWER (*spotting a 'thermal'*): What does the PTA do?
APPLICANT: Oh, a lot. Fund raising for the kids' swimming pool. We organized a fete. I'm a pretty keen swimmer myself.

The 'thermal' has given a number of leads:

The applicant is a family man.
He cares about his children's education.
Does he get involved in other community activities?
Does he take a part in organizing them?
What other hobbies has he?
What can we learn about him from these?
As a member of the PTA how does he act? Is he a rebel or an organizer?

Once you get the conversation going you can follow up leads to cover the points on which you need information, such as whether he is a good organizer, what his motivation is, and whether he is constructive in his criticisms of authority. You steer the conversation when you are under way. (It's hard to move the wheel if you aren't rolling.)

Here is another example:

APPLICANT: I did quite well at British Products Ltd. A couple of things I did turned out very well there.

INTERVIEWER (*spotting a note of pride*): What were these successes you had?

APPLICANT: Well, the first break came when . . .

(The interviewer just listens, putting in a word of encouragement here and there. Success No. 1 takes about five minutes to describe, discuss and comment approvingly upon)

INTERVIEWER: You mentioned a couple of successes. What was the other one?

APPLICANT: Yes, the other project was . . .

(This one is developed in a similar way)

Ask questions to enable him to talk about himself and his interests, but avoid leading questions. For example, in interviewing a mechanic you would not say 'Our mechanics have to work pretty hard and spend a lot of time travelling. I take it you won't mind that?' Most applicants will give you the answer you want to hear. Leading questions are a waste of time, and their answers mislead you. A better way of arriving at the information you want is to say 'How demanding was your last job?' 'How many hours did you work each day, or each week, on average?' Questions beginning WHY, HOW or WHAT always invite a more complete answer, because they cannot be answered with a YES or NO.

Follow up

After the interview, sum up the applicant's qualifications and experience and see whether they match the *man specification*.

Avoid being prejudiced and don't look for somebody who is a replica of the previous holder of the job.

Make up your mind. Is he definitely the person for the job, a possible, or definitely not the right one? Always take up references, especially if you need evidence of particular qualities

Will he be a square peg in a square hole?

which a previous employer would be in a position to tell you about. A telephone conversation with his previous boss will tell you much more than a written reference. Ask the questions listed in the record of telephone reference, Fig. 3.5.

Let him know the result of the interview as soon as possible. Every interview should build good public relations for your company, regardless of the outcome of the application.

Many companies have a much greater turnover than they realize—probably half the women and a quarter of their men are leaving every year often as a result of haphazard selection.

Even people in semi-skilled jobs who are recruited, trained and then leave, represent a dead loss of at least £300 to the company. By playing your part in the selection procedure you can save your company a great deal of trouble, inconvenience, and disappointment.

Fig. 3.5. Record of telephone reference

Name of applicant...

Position wanted...

Previous employer:

Company name...

Address...

....

Contact...
              (name)   (title)

Introduce yourself, explain why you are telephoning and what position the candidate is applying for.
(The person giving the reference will probably ask for your number and call you back.)

Your pattern of questions could be something like this:

1. When did he start and finish his employment with you?

....

2. What was his job? Did he change jobs within the organization? Why?

. . . .

. . . .

3. What positions did he hold?

. . . .

4. How well did he work?

. . . .

5. What is his attitude to hard work?

. . . .

6. Did he lose any time because of poor health?   YES   NO

   For other reasons?   YES   NO

   Notes:. . . . .

   . . . .

7. What sort of timekeeper was he?

   . . . .

8. How did he get along with others?

   . . . .

9. How well do you think he would fill our post? Would the job conditions and circumstances present any problems for him?

   . . . .

   . . . .

10. Why did he leave your company?

   . . . .

11. Would you re-employ him? YES NO If not, why not?

....

12. What are his strong points?

....

What are his weak points?

13. Other information:

....

....

....

....

Note: Telephone references should only be taken up if the applicant knows and approves.

Fig. 3.6. Checklist on your selection procedures

Questions	√ ×	*Notes*
1. Do you always write a job specification and a man specification so that you know what kind of person you are looking for?		
2. Do you ask applicants to fill in an application form and make time to study it before the interview?		
3. Do *you* interview people who are going to work for you before the company engages them?		
4. Have you received training in interview techniques?		
5. Do you use aptitude tests whenever possible?		
6. Do you ask the applicant's permission to seek a previous employer's reference, and obtain this on the telephone whenever possible?		

Questions

1. Prepare a job specification and a man specification for a driver (company light van).

2. Do you think that the immediate superior (section head, supervisor) of the prospective new employee should be involved in the selection procedure?

4. *Introducing the new employee*

Induction is the process of assimilating a new employee into the company and helping him to become an effective and cooperative producer as soon as possible. He may be a youngster just out of school, or a mature man who has worked elsewhere before. Whoever he is, the way in which you treat him for the first week will exert a strong influence on whether he stays with your firm or goes, and if he stays, whether his attitude is one of cooperation or distrust.

Try to make him feel at home and interest him in his job, the department and the company. Some firms go to considerable trouble to arrange for new employees to be shown around and to demonstrate the part their department plays in manufacturing the final product. Most are convinced that good induction reduces staff turnover.

It is a mistake to think that if the personnel department or the welfare officer or training manager have talks with the newcomer, this is all that is needed to help him settle in. Some consider that if there is a company rule book, all you need to do is hand him that to read. They overlook the fact that to new employees the supervisor represents the company and it is he who will exert the biggest single influence on their attitudes.

As a supervisor you must take an interest in every beginner in your department, regardless of whether he has been given the routine reception by personnel department. You yourself do not have to tell him all he needs to know, of course, but it is important that you should ensure that somebody does.

Many supervisors take the new employee to one side for twenty minutes on his first day and deal with the following

Don't try to tell him too much at once

points. They are careful to put across the most important things first and not to tell him too much at once. You may like to use these checklists next time you interview a new starter.

What he will need to know

Company information

Name.
Organization.
Products—how they are made, used and serviced.
Customers.
Managers' names.
Employees.

Departmental information

What it makes.
Where it fits.
Jobs.
Organization.
Supervision—names.
Employees.
Departmental rules.
Breaks: tea, meals.

Where his job fits in

His responsibilities, duties, and job aims.

Pay and hours

Rate: deductions, queries.
Pay: when and how.
Bonus: production, annual.
Hours: overtime, weekends, shifts, clocking.

Services, welfare and amenities

Holidays and holiday pay.
Sickness: notification, certificate.

Pension scheme, if any.
Sick club.
Savings club.
Telephone calls.
Further education.
Canteen.
Toilets and cloakrooms.
Overalls.
Protective clothing.
Sports/social club.

Standards

Efficiency.
Quality.
Safety.
Good housekeeping.
Absenteeism.
Lateness.
Smoking.
Cooperation.
Discipline.
Expectations: what you expect from him, what he can expect from you.

Personal relationships

Help and cooperation.
Assure him that you will back him up.
Encourage him to come to you with his problems.
Tell him that he is joining a team and will have cooperation from his fellow members.

Requests.
Time off.
Promotion.

Miscellaneous
Travelling.

Fire precautions.
Other rules and traditions.
Trade union.
Length of notice.
Grievance procedure, especially first step.

Note: The Contracts of Employment Act requires that within 13 weeks of starting he should be given much of this information in writing, so be sure that this is not overlooked.

Useful items for you to know

His experience, including any evidence of leadership experience.
Where he worked before.
His likes and dislikes.
Hobbies and sports.
Family.
Friends and acquaintances in the firm.
How far away he lives and how he gets to work.

Some people like to keep themselves to themselves. so be tactful and do not go beyond a friendly interest—make it a conversation not an inquisition.

These points will not all have the same importance. Some *must* be covered, others *should* be if possible, but others are just background information. Certain items will not apply at all. It is a good idea to grade this information in your mind, so that you do not waste instruction time on items in the third category when you should be ensuring that all first category information has been given.

Do not waste time on the outer ring until you have dealt with the bullseye.

When you have your talk with the new man, put him at his ease, welcome him promptly in a friendly way, and get his name right. Tell him what he can call you—some supervisors find it a good idea to get that in before anybody else does. Find out if he knows anybody in the company. If he has never been to work

Do not waste time on the outer ring until you have dealt with the bullseye

before, remember that it is difficult making the changeover from school to work because of the totally different circumstances to be found there. Here are just some of the differences:

School	*Work*
Only six hours a day.	Forty hour week and perhaps
Three months' holiday a year.	three weeks' holiday.
More variety of activity—different classes, games, etc.	Probably less varied activities.
More changes of workplace.	Usually in one spot.
Companions of same age and outlook.	Companions of all ages, not so easy to communicate with.
Little danger of accidents.	Hazards.
Constant development of the individual.	Development of the individual not the prime aim.

These two lists clearly show that the transition from school to work involves the youngster in a drastic readjustment and needs to be handled with consideration on your part.

Whether he is a youngster or not, see that the new man is told all the things he needs to know for his physical and social comfort, e.g., welfare facilities, tea and lunch breaks, washrooms, and where to hang his coat. Make sure that he knows all about timekeeping, overtime and how he is paid. Introduce him to your deputy and the people he will be working with, not forgetting the union representative if you have one. Many supervisors put newcomers with a person who has the right attitude to his job and is of a friendly disposition, and of a similar age group, at least not old enough to be his grandfather. If you don't already do this, try it.

Where induction ends and job training begins

Induction is the reception of a new member of staff into the company, while training is the sequel—the process of imparting the knowledge and skills needed for the job. Some new starters are already competent and need no training, but others will need instruction. Your company may have a training centre for new entrants and in this case you will have few worries as long as you maintain close cooperation with it. Quite a number of supervisors, however, find that they themselves are responsible for seeing that training is done on the job. Don't just leave the new employee to watch an experienced one, because he will pick up all his mistakes, and learning by watching and then copying by trial and error is very wasteful.

If your department is a large one and you supervise so many people that you do not normally have time to maintain a regular personal contact, make a point of seeing your new man, say one week after he joins. By then he will have settled down and there will inevitably be queries and small problems to sort out for him. Even if there are not, he will certainly appreciate your interest.

Managers and supervisors who take pains to help new staff to adjust themselves to their new working environment, find that their trouble is amply repaid in reduced staff turnover and in improved cooperation. So next time a new employee comes along, take the opportunity of laying the foundations for a long and mutually profitable partnership between him and the company by giving systematic and friendly attention.

Fig. 4.1. Checklist on your induction procedure

Questions	$\times \sqrt{}$	*Notes*
1. Do you have few new people leaving within weeks of joining your department?		
2. Do you spend at least 15 minutes getting to know every new employee?		
3. Do you plan what you are going to tell him and ask him?		
4. Do new staff tend to settle down quickly in your department, making friends easily?		
5. Have all your staff had the opportunity of going all round the company to see what goes on outside their own part of it?		
6. Does anybody teach a new person the job or do they just 'pick it up'?		
7. Do you make a point of seeing new starters about one week later to ask if they have any problems?		
8. Do you never find breaches of regulations which have occurred through ignorance?		
9. What special steps do you take to help school leavers to adjust to your department?		
10. What special steps do you take to help newly appointed supervisors to adjust to your department?		
11. Do you ensure that they are given the information required by the Contracts of Employment Act, etc.?		

Questions	× √	Notes
12. Do you carry out a simplified form of induction procedure for staff who are transferred to your department?		

Questions

1. To what extent do you consider good induction can improve morale in the factory?

2. To what extent should the supervisor become involved in the induction process?

3. Imagine that you have just started in a new job. Describe your feelings, and what help, advice, information, etc., you would want from your new boss in your first week.

5. *Your responsibility for training*

Since a supervisor is responsible for his department's output, he must also make himself responsible for the competence and ability of his staff. This means that he must diagnose training needs and make arrangements to satisfy them.

He should concern himself about training:

himself.
subordinate supervisors.
the non-supervisory staff of his department.

How to develop your own ability

Your capacity to do your present job depends on what you are expected to achieve and how your abilities measure up to these demands. It is important that you should know what is expected of you, and try to put down on paper the terms of reference of the position you occupy. Then you have to take stock of your knowledge, skill and qualifications and see where, if at all, they fall short of what is needed.

But training to do your present job better is not the only kind of development possible. There are a great many other ways in which you can increase your scope and calibre. A growing number of supervisors are undergoing courses for the Certificate of the National Examinations Board in Supervisory Studies. The syllabus requires 240 hours of education (often with day release, spread over a year). This illustrates the amount of time and effort which many companies consider it reasonable to devote to supervisory development.

The following list of suggestions is intended to provide ideas for improvement in your present job and growth potential for your future career.

1. Reading: Ask to be put on the company's circulation list for trade and technical magazines. The quarterly magazine of the Institute of Supervisory Management contains some very good articles.

   Look for management books in your local library. I can recommend the following:

   What Every Supervisor Should Know, L. Bittel, McGraw-Hill.
   The Techniques of Delegating, Laird, McGraw-Hill.
   How Foremen Can Control Costs, Phil Carroll, McGraw-Hill.
   Work Study, R. M. Currie, Pitman.
   Supervisory Studies, P. W. Betts, Macdonald & Evans Ltd.

2. Join professional bodies in your field.
3. Join management and supervisory discussion groups.
4. Attend courses, seminars, conferences.
5. Obtain the prospectus of your local technical college.
6. Learn all you can from the sales representatives who visit your company on behalf of suppliers of equipment, tools and techniques. Although they are there to sell rather than educate, they do provide valuable leads about the latest developments.
7. Watch out for TV and radio programmes on management.
8. Attend a work study appreciation course.
9. Managers are going to need the following skills to an increasing degree, and courses are available in all of them:
   ▷ Problem analysis and decision making
   ▷ Interviewing (discipline, grievance, advice, selection, appraisal)
   ▷ Conducting a meeting (e.g., discussion with subordinates)
   ▷ Putting a case or argument.

Take advantage of your company's training and development programme

Show that you are interested. Your chief, the personnel manager and training director, are ready to help managers who want to help themselves. Don't be ashamed to ask for help or

feel that you'll be revealing a secret weakness. One of the necessary qualities of an executive is the ability for self-analysis and the determination to improve.

Where can you go for outside help and guidance on suitable courses?

Management Training Consultants,
214 Saint Nicholas Circle, Leicester.
Tel. Leicester 27062.

The British Institute of Management,
Management House, Parker Street, London WC2.
Tel. 01-405 3456.

The Industrial Society,
48 Bryanston Square, London W1.
Tel. 01-262 2401

The Institute of Supervisory Management,
22 Bore Street, Lichfield, Staffordshire.
Tel. Lichfield 51346.

Your own industry's Industrial Training Board.

What subjects are covered in supervisory training programmes?

The following list is almost a complete inventory, and it is therefore unlikely that all items would be relevant to any one supervisor, but it shows you what the field covers.

1. The main areas of management knowledge (i.e., a frame of reference for the science/art of management).
2. Training Within Industry for supervisors (job relations, job methods, job instruction, job safety).
3. Qualities of a good supervisor.
4. Human relations: Leadership, morale, motivation, induction, giving orders and directions, correcting and improving employees, supervising women, handling complaints and grievances, human problems at work (case studies), resistance to change, communication (need for and organizing of) including chain of command (briefing groups) consultation, representative systems, employee opinion surveys, suggestion schemes and mass media, sensitivity training—'T' groups—group dynamics.
5. Systems of payment: Individual incentive schemes, group incentive schemes, job evaluation and merit rating.
6. Administration of the job.
   Effective job organization: Budgeting time, scheduling work,

delegating, planning, critical path or network analysis, records, procedures, systems.

Training and employee development: Departmental training, individual training, talent spotting, guiding subordinate supervisors, management succession and career development, problem analysis and decision making, the union contract, selecting staff.

7. Principles of organization: Relationships within an organization—line, staff, functional, lateral, position descriptions and terms of reference, authority and responsibility, delegation and completed staff work, spans of control, unity of command versus functional multiple direction from a team of specialists.

8. The tool subjects: Organization and methods/work study, value analysis, the use of statistical controls, etc.

9. Communication skills: Report and letter writing, putting a case, talking to groups of people, conducting a meeting, interviewing (for selection, counselling, grievance, performance review, etc.).

10. The use of service departments: Management accounting, cost accounting, budgetary and cost control, quality control, production control, personnel, training, industrial engineering, O & M/work study, safety, the structure of this company.

11. Background knowledge/general education: Economics, structure of the economy.

Training subordinate supervisors

Everything under the previous heading applies to subordinate supervisors (section leaders who are responsible to you), but in addition you need to do the following.

1. Define, for each supervisor, his particular goals, and provide the resources necessary for achieving them.

2. Periodically discuss progress towards these goals and give help and guidance where needed.

3. Use him as the main line of communication to the staff and

Training your subordinate supervisors

encourage him to come forward with the grievances, questions, and suggestions which his subordinates have raised.

4. Regularly call your supervisor(s) in on informative, consultative, and problem-solving meetings. In-company supervisory training sessions can be arranged in order to improve the supervisor's understanding of his role in the management team and the functions of other departments.

5. Look at the requirements of the job and the knowledge and skills of the supervisor, and when there is a deficiency provide training to remedy it. If he is promotable, the same exercise can be carried out for the next rung of the ladder.

6. Examine the content of any training course intended for the supervisor, briefing him before and debriefing him afterwards so that he can see the relevance of it to his job.

7. Constantly create situations which call for and encourage learning. These include delegation, understudying, project work, committee assignments, guided experience, and planned job rotation.

Delegation

This means allowing people to take decisions and use discretion on your behalf. The chapter entitled 'Don't do it all yourself' gives guidelines on how to go about this. Delegation forces people to make decisions and take responsibility, exercising their knowledge and skill and making them want to learn more so that they can handle these situations.

Understudying

Allow different section leaders or potential supervisors to take over from you when you are away. If you give two or three this opportunity, no one person will take it for granted that he is automatically in line for your job. This keeps several people on their toes, and avoids anyone building up hopes which may not be realized.

Project work

You can set projects for your section leaders which will help you to achieve your own targets and at the same time give them valuable experience.

Here are some projects which have been assigned to staff with this in mind:

Training. Submit a training schedule to ensure sufficient trained staff to give adequate coverage of all jobs in the event of sickness.

Safety. Work out an inspection schedule to cover all danger points. Prepare a safety talk for the operators in the department.

Cost Control. Study the waste problem and make recommendations.

Quality Control. Plan a departmental Q & R campaign.

Stores. Work out a better stock control and reordering system.

It is most important that project work assigned as a method of staff development should in fact be properly completed and the end product *utilized*. Frustration and resentment can build up if the hard work put into a project is disregarded or shelved.

Committee assignments

Encourage subordinate supervisors to sit on committees dealing with safety, welfare, industrial relations, etc. Ask whether the section leader can accompany you when the boss calls a meeting.

Guided experience

Take a particular weakness of one of your subordinates, diagnose the cause and deliberately plan with him how to give him training and experience which will eliminate the defect.

For example, he may be careless in filling in some of the information on production control documents. You identify this as a failure to realize its importance; and a half day in the production control office trying to read his own writing or guess at missing facts will make him careful in future.

Job rotation

This means allowing a section head to take charge of another section while someone else looks after his own. This kind of sideways move should not occur too often, and it is not advisable to switch people around unless they are going to benefit from it (e.g., if they are in line for promotion and will need broad experience).

Job rotation is helpful in some ways, but presents problems unless done carefully. It has advantages and limitations which you should bear in mind before adopting it.

Advantages of job rotation

1. Rotation broadens an individual's experience.
2. It tests staff by exposing them to different problems.
3. It gives new challenges and interests to people who may be in a rut.
4. It brings new brains to old jobs. A person probably runs out of improvement ideas after a few years in a job.
5. It brings in outside experience.

6. Rotation keeps interest alive when there are no immediate prospects of advancement.
7. Staff can try several jobs and find their true niche.

Job rotation

Limitations of job rotation

1. Rotations upset routine. The job could be jeopardized by transferring a successful man and trying one who is an unknown quantity.
2. Change can be a bore, too.

3. Top management must ensure that everybody understands what is going on, otherwise staff will become insecure and lose confidence in themselves, thinking they have failed and are being pushed aside.
4. The employee may become insecure if his bosses are playing musical chairs.
5. It is important that the previous supervisor's back-up man should be a good man technically and practically if the new boss is not himself experienced in the department's work.

The benefits of conducting briefing groups (departmental meetings):

1. They give out information.
2. They explain reasons for changes, policies, etc.
3. They make clear who is responsible for what.
4. They encourage analytical thought.
5. They create a sense of involvement (team).
6. They give staff a sense of status.
7. Staff learn your way of thinking.

The benefits of the morning inspection:

1. It identifies problems, personal and production, so that people can get on with the job.
2. It settles people down to work.
3. It enables you to give a word of encouragement or praise.
4. It maintains standards of safety, good housekeeping, quality.
5. It enables you to spot potential bottlenecks, such as staff shortages and machine breakdowns.
6. It provides an opportunity to reinforce the authority of your deputy.

Training non-supervisory staff

Most supervisors have their share of novices to guide along the right lines or staff with experience elsewhere, who must be instructed in the company's special work methods. If you see that your staff are well trained you will find that there is less turnover, waste and injury, greater efficiency and the improved morale which comes of knowing the job and knowing that the supervisor is interested in one's ability to do it. Whether or not you are expected to do the teaching yourself it is important for you to understand the main principles of instructing, because you can then either act as tutor or delegate the job of teaching while knowing how to ensure that it is properly carried out.

Supervisors sometimes fail in their responsibility for training operators. The most common mistake is to leave an employee to learn a job by observing somebody else. Another is to put the trainee with the wrong sort of tutor, somebody who is perhaps very good at the job, but has no idea how to explain it to somebody else, or if he knows, perhaps he has no inclination to do so.

Some supervisors are unaware of the problems of learning and will write a person off as hopeless if he does not pick up the job very quickly. In fact, he may be quite intelligent but may not learn the knack at once, or, if he is an immigrant, his inadequate knowledge of the language may prove an obstacle.

It helps to remember that:

TEACHING = HELPING PEOPLE TO LEARN

This statement looks so obvious that it seems hardly worth making and yet very many people pride themselves on having given a very fine lesson regardless of whether the pupil derived any benefit from it. The emphasis in teaching must be put in the right place: it is how much the learner learns that really matters, not how much knowledge the teacher propagates. The Training Within Industry people expressed it in this way: 'If the pupil hasn't learnt the teacher hasn't taught.'

There are eight principles which can be applied in nearly every case when there is teaching to be done. They have proved their validity over and over again by helping people to learn faster and more completely a wide range of different jobs. For convenience we will suppose that you are doing the teaching, although in practice you will probably often delegate the job to somebody else. (If you do, why not lend him this book to read up these tips?)

Stimulate the learner's interest

The instructor's attitude counts. Even the dullest routine can be made more interesting with a spark of imagination.

It is up to you to find out what is the mainspring of the newcomer's interest in the job, so that you can use its power from the very start. Earning power usually ranks very high but don't overlook the less apparent but no less important reasons— pride in the finished article, job satisfaction, and the need that most of us feel, to be good at what we do. Perhaps he does not realize the full scope of what can be achieved through the skill he is going to acquire. It is important to encourage his enthusiasm from the start. Know him and understand his aims, so that you can tie them in with achievable objectives.

Sustain his interest

It is a common phenomenon among people learning something new that their interest tends to flag after the first three or four attempts. Partly this is because they could make great progress at the start, but now their rate of learning appears to be slowing down. They have probably reached the stage of sheer hard work, uninteresting practice, memorizing. There may even be a sense of slipping back—of being less skilful at the beginning of this lesson than they were at the end of the last one.

This stage, which is well known and recognized by education psychologists is sometimes called a *learning plateau*—a point where progress up the mountain seems to have levelled off. A feeling of frustration may set in unless a sense of progress can be maintained—and this, of course, is true of every stage of learning. To achieve a sense of progress a learner needs a target— so much to be learned by such and such a date and he must have evidence or signs that he is moving towards it.

These signs will depend on what you are teaching him. They may be in the form of progress through the instruction manual, periodic trial runs, or being entrusted with progressively more challenging exercises. If you show your interest in his progress his own will increase. Know how far he reached last time you took him, and tell him what you want him to achieve this time. It has been found that most people respond best when they earn approval for a good performance or incur criticism for a bad one. When the instructor says nothing either way, for a long time, they tend to lose interest.

Build his confidence in you and himself

In you:

▷ Aim at the highest standards. Nobody wants to put in an extra effort if the outcome is only going to be a sloppy second-rate performance.
▷ Show him that you know your subject.
▷ Let him see that you have patience.
▷ Show that you have a systematic plan for teaching and that you are using it.

In himself:

▷ Show that you know he can do it. A battle is half won if a man thinks he can win.
▷ Handle his mistakes properly. If he gives the wrong answer to your questions try to see why he answered in that way. If part of his thinking was correct give him credit for that part when pointing out his mistake.
▷ Keep your temper. If you get angry your pupil will become flustered and nervous, try too hard and make more mistakes.
▷ Give him credit for what knowledge he already has. He may already know a little about your subject and it probably seems quite a lot to him. Many instructors classify such people as know-alls, and try to convince them that they don't know as much as they think they do. This can be very damaging to the learner's morale and quite confusing, unless the existing knowledge is reconciled with what you are telling him. It is hard sometimes to resist telling a trainee that what he learns on day-release is all right in theory, but doesn't work in practice. Be patient and try to explain why this is so.

Don't get angry if he makes mistakes

Prepare your instruction in advance

What you need to say. Decide on the priorities. In any subject there are sections which it is vital for the learner to know—facts without which there can be no understanding of the subject at all. These can be called primary items. There are also secondary items which you would like to teach him, incidental pieces of information which are not essential. Make sure that if time is limited you do not miss out the essential facts through spending time on the secondary ones.

Break the job into steps. Ask yourself: what do I do first? then, what comes next? and so on until you have the job broken down into separate stages, none of them so long that the learner has difficulty in remembering. A good example can be found in the telephone kiosk where dialling instructions are published like this:

Have your money ready.
Lift the telephone.
Dial when you hear the dialling tone.
When you hear rapid pips put a coin in.
Speak.

Teaching aids. Make sure that you have close at hand any tools or instruments, books or illustrations which you will need to use for demonstration.

Let him have a try under your guidance

The trial run is a very important part of the learning process because while the learner is practising he is recalling what you have told and shown him. The act of recalling is an essential part of learning. It helps, when conditions permit, to ask the learner to explain what he is doing as he goes through the job the first time. By repeating in this way what you have told him, he fixes the lesson more securely in his mind. Equally important, the trial run provides you with an opportunity of correcting any errors he may make. It is advisable to continue with as many trial runs as necessary until the job is performed without a single mistake.

For safety's sake, do everything possible to remove from the job any hazards which might endanger him.

When you teach, tell and show

It has been proved by experiment that when you *tell* and *show* a person how to do a new job this is very much more effective than when you just tell or just show. Telling is not enough. It is important to show the acting pilot officer which is the ejection seat button, not just to tell him. Showing is not enough. Nobody would sit a learner next to a concert pianist and expect him to learn by observation how to play the instrument. The machinery in your department can be just as baffling to the novice, so

I must remember to *show* the next one

remember that besides seeing and practising there must be a proper explanation.

Ask him questions so that you can be sure that he has understood

There are two levels of technical learning. A trainee can be shown how to perform a certain sequence of actions which will give an end result, and yet never understand how the result is achieved. This is the shallower level of learning and it does enable the person to cope with events as long as everything goes smoothly. The deeper level of learning combines understanding and memory together so that the learner understands the underlying principle and sees through the job. Because he understands, he can improvise and use his initiative when things go wrong.

Whenever somebody needs to have this second type of knowledge, which one might call *insight*, you should ask him questions during or after his trial run stage. You might ask 'Why do you think this happens?' 'How do you think it works?' or 'What do you think would happen if such and such a step were missed out?'. These questions leading into a discussion will develop real understanding.

Revise

How soon do people forget what they learn? Research has shown that one hour after a lesson, people are likely to forget over half of what they learned during it. The following table tells you more about how much people tend to forget:

Time interval since learning	% forgotten
$\frac{1}{3}$ hour	42
1 hour	56
8 hours	64
1 day	66
2 days	72
6 days	75

We know that the learner has constantly to be reminded of the important things or he will forget. Many instructors surmount this problem by assigning certain exercises to be carried out whenever time permits. If you are unable to do this, make a time allowance at the beginning of your second lesson to go over again the main points he should recall from the first.

Practice. The most effective sort of revision is practice on the job, so give the learner as much opportunity as you can to exercise his newly-acquired skills and knowledge by doing the job himself.

Make a training plan for individuals

Ideally every employee's training needs should be analysed by specifying what he should know, what he does know, and therefore what he still has to learn. This may be too large a task to tackle in the short term. So begin with your key personnel, those whose jobs are critical to the quality and speed of the department's work.

If you look at the individual training needs analysis form in Fig. 5.1 you will see how to specify the items which the employee has to know or do. Then there is a column for whether his knowledge and ability for each item is adequate or improvable and then the third column is for specifying the training needs.

Figure 5.2 shows an individual employee training schedule sheet, which is the sequel to the analysis mentioned above. On it you can schedule the target date for whatever training you have prescribed, and also note down where and how he is going to be given the required instruction.

Make a training plan for the department

Suppose that, as happens in many departments, a supervisor has a certain number of staff and a certain number of jobs, and he wants to train everybody so that they are versatile enough to tackle several kinds of work, thus covering the department in case of sickness, resignation, or a special rush job requiring an all-out effort by everybody.

Fig. 5.1. Individual training needs analysis (for present job)

Name..

Job title..

Responsible to..

Supervises...

1. DUTIES (general description of the scope of his responsibilities)

2. SPECIFIC DUTIES ITEM	Adequate	Improvable	TRAINING NEEDED

Fig. 5.2. Individual employee training schedule

Name...

Job title...

Responsible to.....................................

Training item	Target date	Comments

One way of planning a training timetable to meet this need is to square off a sheet of paper, as shown in Fig 5.3, putting jobs along the top and employees down the side.

You tick off who can do which jobs and this shows you at a glance those operations for which you are short of trained staff. The next step is to mark in your plan the date by which you want to train each person bearing in mind who is leaving, who are the least versatile and ought to be trained first, and what the future workload is going to be. The letter 'T' and a date shows that, for example, Hill must be trained in coding by November 15, to take over from Brown who is leaving. Some trade unions in certain circumstances may not want to go along with having full interchangeability between jobs, but if you lay your cards on the table and point out the advantages to their members, such as security, pay and so on, and at the same time you try to meet the union's objections, the chances are that they will cooperate.

There is surely no more practical way of developing good relations in your department than by showing your concern for the staff and their security through the medium of an effective training policy.

Fig. 5.3. Stores administration section training plan

Dept: Stores Section: Admin.	Invoices	Coding	Inventory	Issues	Remarks
Brown	√	√	√	√	Leaving firm 30/Nov.
Hill	√	T 15/Nov.		√	
Charles	T 30/Nov.		T 30/Nov.	√	
Cross			T 15/Nov.	T 15/Dec.	
Smith	T 7/Nov.	T 30/Nov.	T 15/Dec.		Joins firm 1/Nov.
Notes on workload			Stock-taking Dec.		

Fig. 5.4. Checklist on training

Questions	× √	Notes
1. Do new recruits rapidly become producers?		
2. If you delegate to somebody else the training of a member of your team, do you still continue to show your interest in his progress?		
3. Have you a training plan for your successor and is it being followed?		
4. In the absence of any one of your employees, is there someone capable of doing his job?		
5. Are people in your section capable of doing more than one job?		
6. Do your experienced staff know how to instruct?		
7. Do you know how to instruct?		
8. Do you prepare a job breakdown (very simple instruction manual) for the jobs you most frequently have to teach?		
9. Has your department a good safety record?		
10. Does your department use materials economically (therefore skilfully)?		
11. Do you analyse a person's mistakes with him in an encouraging way?		
12. Does the department continue to function smoothly in your absence?		
13. Are all of your staff as efficient as their age and length of service should indicate?		

Questions

1. Some supervisors assume that if a new and inexperienced employee sits next to an old hand he ought to be able to learn the job through observation. How successful is this method of imparting knowledge and how do you think it can be improved upon?

2. What are the benefits of effective training
   (a) to the firm,
   (b) to you,
   (c) to the person being trained?

3. ' "Training is the training officer's job" is only partly true.' Give your comments.

6. *Understanding complaints and grievances*

Have you ever thought about the difference between a complaint and a grievance? These words seem to mean almost the same thing, but I should like to draw a distinction between the two. A complaint occurs when somebody tells you about his dissatisfaction or problem. The grievance, on the other hand, is the dissatisfaction itself. The complaint is the effect and the grievance is the cause. Many people have grievances which they never express in words but they have other ways of expressing them. Sometimes a person's work will deteriorate in quantity or quality, he may become moody or depressed, or cause dissatisfaction among those around him. His preoccupation may make him become inattentive or careless, so that an accident occurs, or he may leave his job altogether to try and escape the cause of his trouble. We could express this cause-and-effect relationship as shown overleaf in Fig. 6.1.

If there is no complaint the supervisor may not realize that there is a problem at all and simply attribute these effects to modern lackadaisical attitudes. But a complaint gives him something to go on, something to account for the drop in productivity and to show that action needs to be taken to put it right, so a complaint is the supervisor's ally and ought not to exasperate him. If he is receptive, he may receive more grumbles but they are less likely to be serious ones.

Fig. 6.1

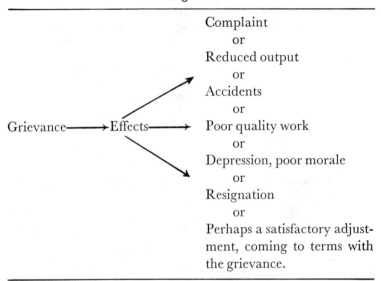

Complaint
or
Reduced output
or
Accidents
or
Grievance——→Effects——→ Poor quality work
or
Depression, poor morale
or
Resignation
or
Perhaps a satisfactory adjustment, coming to terms with the grievance.

Complaints are not always to be taken at their face value

Though complaints show that something is wrong, they do not always tell you accurately what the trouble is.

A man may let off steam by complaining about the tools he has to work with, when what is really bothering him is the fact that he thinks his supervisor has favourites. Home problems can cause trouble at work so that a normally cooperative and steady employee flies off the handle for no apparent reason until you find that he hasn't slept for three nights as a result of the baby's night-time feeding troubles; and most wives will expect dad to be especially outspoken if he slips on a roller skate in the front garden after having a bad day at the office. Avoid being inquisitive about an employee's personal affairs but don't go to the other extreme. Some supervisors take the attitude: 'I'm not concerned with people's personal problems. They can leave them at the gate when they clock on and pick them up again when they go home.' It would be very convenient if we could all switch our troubles off and on like that, but of course we can't.

There are many things that make people disguise their

A bad day at the office makes things worse

troubles. Sometimes they do so because their real grievance puts them in an unfavourable light or makes them look absurd or they may be afraid to admit it even to themselves, or the true problem may be so complex that it defies definition. This means that the supervisor has to diagnose the grievance and see what lies behind the apparent problem. This diagnosis is not so difficult if you remember that our grievances exist in the gap or deficit between what we want and what we are getting. When

Diagnose the grievance

we believe that we are being denied those things we have a right to, a grievance results. We may be denied the things we need in our workplace—such as a reasonable wage, satisfying work, security, adequate equipment, companionship, good working conditions and a reasonable boss. On the other hand, our grievances may have nothing to do with work at all. We need health, a happy and tranquil home life, three square meals a day, hobbies and time to enjoy them, a pleasant home and a chance to give the children at least as good a start in life as we had. If any of these hopes is not fulfilled a feeling of deprivation may cause a grievance.

To spot an employee's problem the supervisor must be able to see in what way life is dealing him out less than he hopes to get, for in that gap between his aspirations and reality lies the root of his discontent. The problem is that, as stated in chapter 1, not everybody has the same needs. In some measure we all want certain things, but not with the same intensity. The young man often looks for more money before security of employment; the extrovert wants company, while another will sacrifice anything else for the satisfaction of having a job he likes doing. So it all boils down to knowing your staff. Be interested in what they want and, as far as you can, help them to achieve it through their work. Commonsense warns against giving anybody advice and judgement on personal or private matters, but if an employee seeks your guidance you can either help him to think matters out for himself, or you can put him in contact with the appropriate organization—for example, the Citizen's Advice Bureau, or your personnel department (if you have one).

Five rules for grievance interviews

It is not always possible, of course, to know all the staff working under you. We are moved around and so are those whom we supervise, and the sheer number of people some of us have to control makes it difficult to know more than their names. This is where the five rules come in. They are a guide to anyone who has to interview a person with a grievance and they almost invariably uncover the root of the problem.

Rule 1. Listen and do not interrupt

The employee is probably tense and all wound up with his complaint, so let him get it off his chest. Don't correct him on points of detail even if they are inaccurate—let him present his whole case. You may later have to put him right about inaccuracies, but wait until the end. By letting him talk you have not conceded anything which you may later regret.

Rule 2. Show interest

Have you ever told your grievance to somebody who fiddled about in his filing cabinet, yawned, made an irrelevant telephone call, and kept looking at his watch? The individual's grievance is the most important thing in the world to him, so try to look at it as if it were your own and show real interest.

Rule 3. Do not get drawn into an argument

This is easier said than done, but if you follow Rule 1 an argument is less likely to develop. If you should come to a stalemate amounting to a 'yes, I did—no, you didn't' deadlock, try another tack.

Rule 4. Repeat back in your own words what he has said

By stating his problem in your own words you ensure that you have understood the story correctly, and you prove that you have listened. This leaves no doubt as to your attentiveness, and helps him to agree with at least something you are saying, and to consider his problem objectively. Many people who are unwilling to come straight out with their real grievances try out the supervisor's receptiveness with a side issue first. If that is sympathetically received they bring out the real problem.

Rule 5. Beware of promises

An obvious one this. Do remember not to make any promises which you cannot keep.

Not only do these five rules enable you to come to grips with the real hidden problem if there is one, but they also have a useful side-effect. You will find that even if, despite all your efforts at finding a solution to the person's problem, it is impossible to solve it for him, you will nevertheless have lessened his grievance. There is something about the process of sharing a problem with another person, defining it, appreciating it and trying to do something about it, which reduces its severity—a secret which, no doubt, is at least as old as the confession box.

To summarize:

1. Don't repress complaints.
2. Don't always take them at their face value. There may be something behind them.
3. You will understand grievances better if you understand your staff, what each wants out of life, and where their hopes are not being realized.
4. Use the five rules for dealing with complaints.

The grievance procedure

In most companies, and almost invariably where there is a union, there is a right and wrong way for staff to raise any complaints they have. It's important for you to find out, if you do not already know, what the right way is. Your personnel officer or, if you do not have one, your general manager or works manager will be able to tell you. The usual sequence is as follows:

1. The employee with a complaint takes it to his supervisor.
2. If he is not satisfied with the result, he takes it to the union representative who in turn takes it up again with the supervisor.
3. If no settlement results, the union representative takes it up with higher management.

It is important to insist on the fact that an employee should himself approach you, as his supervisor, in the first instance and not ask his representative to do so. You should also try to persuade the representative to see the wisdom of this. Most problems do not warrant his intervention; he is there in reserve for those that do. The exception to this rule is when the problem is one that affects everybody, such as car parks or canteens— then naturally the union representative will take it up because he is the legitimate spokesman for the staff as a whole.

If individual complaints are constantly short-circuiting the supervisor and going straight to the union representative, it could be that the supervisor is not very approachable and in that case he should polish up on his five rules.

Fig. 6.2. Checklist on handling complaints and grievances

Questions	× √	Notes
1. Do you make time at the earliest opportunity to listen when there is the slightest hint of a grievance?		
2. Do you find a suitable time and place?		
3. Do you show real undivided interest?		
4. If the union representative raises an individual's problem which is new to you, do you tactfully remind him that the employee should have come to you about it first?		
5. Do you avoid a sterile argument?		
6. Do you summarize his complaint(s) in order to check with him the accuracy of your interpretation?		
7. Are you careful not to give a promise when you are not sure you can fulfil it?		

Questions

1. As a supervisor you find that the union representative is taking employees' grievances to your department head and by-passing you. What steps can you take to prevent this happening?

2. What rules do you think apply to grievance interviewing?

3. What kinds of emotional problems do employees sometimes have to face at work?

4. An employee is frightened of losing his job, and this insecurity is affecting his work. How would you deal with this situation?

7. Introducing changes

Changes are occurring so fast nowadays that your company is probably employing techniques, tools and machinery that were not even invented five years ago, and it is certain that the next five years will bring even greater innovations. Machines and systems respond quickly to changes and do not groan very much at the introduction of them, but people are different. One eminent doctor and philosopher advances the theory that it is the failure of our organism to respond to modern life in appropriate ways which produces so much mental ill-health and so much physical sickness with psychological origins. We cannot easily adapt to new circumstances and new ways of doing things. Our reaction when faced with them is often one of fear and obstructiveness.

Why should this be so? One of the main reasons for resistance to new ideas is the fact that they appear to be a criticism of the old way of doing things. The need to innovate is taken to mean that something was wrong with the old way and by implication with those who were using it. Then there is the fear of the unknown. 'What are these changes going to be, and what effect will they have on me?' people want to know, for many are afraid of being unable to cope with a new set-up, and of being criticized for doing the job wrongly. 'Will I look a fool for not catching on quickly? Will some of these youngsters be doing the job better than I can?' The old rut is comfortable and it hurts to move out of it, especially if you are no longer young and think that you might be on the scrap heap before long under the new scheme of things.

There is also the fact that changes often break up people's

Will I look a fool?

groupings, separating friends and putting them with people they know less well—perhaps even isolating them altogether.

A shoe-making firm changed over one of its factories from batch production to flow-line production some years ago. Under the old batch-production system the girls used to sit facing each other round a table, an arrangement which permitted them to exchange views and jokes together. Then came the flow-line arrangement which made it impossible to do this because an operator could only see the backs of the people in front and one person on each side if she turned her head. People felt badly about it at first and even now at tea breaks when the girls are free to have a talk they tend to seek out those same people with whom they formerly worked on batch production. It shows how much people like to stay together, and resist the break-up of their groups.

There may be a loss of earnings as a result of the new way of doing the job, or perhaps the money may be better but one's skill becomes redundant. Many shorthand-typists will not accept work as copy typists because they do not want to lose their shorthand. Again, though a person is no worse off himself, others who were below him in status or skill have now caught up with him because of the new technologies which have done away with the advantages that skills used to confer. This means a loss of economic advantage and a blow to one's self-esteem. Sometimes, although one is prepared to forget all these objections to change and give it a try, a trade union sees real danger and imposes its veto so that solidarity with one's fellow workers forbids acceptance. Resistance to change has always been there, hidden, of course, but whereas in the old days people had to tolerate it in silence, now they can and do express themselves more freely.

How can you get people to accept change?

It is in everybody's interest—management's, the staff's, and the public's who buy the products—that new and better ways should be found and put into effect. The supervisor has a vital part to play in winning the staff's acceptance for new ideas. He is paid by the firm to implement top management's policy, and if this includes the adoption of new ideas then these also must be implemented.

It is no use telling people to 'like it or lump it', and neither is it a responsible sort of attitude to say 'It has got to be done in this new way because the boss says so.' Men must be given the reasons for the changes that are being made, and the supervisor has to play his part in putting them across even if he personally doesn't agree with them. This may sound hard, and it may go against the grain to have to advocate something you do not really want, but that is your duty. Privately, out of the staff's hearing, you should put your case to your own superior, giving the reasons why you think the proposed innovation is wrong, but if your opinion is overruled then you must accept that decision. The only alternative to this way of running a business would be to have 'committee management' and this would be far too slow in today's competitive world. The top man, like the referee, has the last word. Those are the rules of the game, so

It's the unexpected that shocks us most

don't be lukewarm about new methods and procedures. Unless you give them your support, you cannot expect the staff to go along with them. Besides not being lukewarm, what else can you do to get people to accept change? And what can top management do?

It is the unexpected which shocks us most. When we know that something is going to happen in six months' time, we accustom ourselves to the thought and make our own private preparations. News of a transfer may mean all sorts of arrangements concerning the house, the children's school, hire purchase and so on. So tell people well in advance of things that will affect them.

Allow people to have their say and report back to management the comments you hear

Management needs to know what the employees say, and they like to know that their comments are being listened to and their feelings considered. When the supervisor won't listen and says with an air of finality 'That's company policy', it can be very frustrating. It is this sort of thing that makes the men go to their union representative, who then goes straight to the top, bypassing the immediate superior. It is true that some managements encourage this by not keeping the supervisor as well informed as they ought, but don't expect to be spoonfed with information all the time. If you don't know, ask.

Don't be shaken by criticism and ridicule. Have determination and a broad back

The management of the Gresham Press at Old Woking had a mural painted on one of their walls as part of a plan to make the working environment more pleasant. There were some humorous remarks about it at first, but here is what one of the firm's supervisors had to say: 'They may make fun of the new picture on the wall, but they are secretly proud of it.' Managing, whether you are a supervisor or a general manager, is a lonely job, and you have to stick to your guns when you know you are in the right.

Try to introduce changes gradually

Some changes can only be made drastically. But most often people will accept gradual change more readily, innovations which are made little by little, so that as one success is scored it provides a basis for acceptance of the next round. Consider whether this can be done in your case. It often gives people time to adapt to the new trends if they are embarked upon in a gradual way. You can make the change in one section, or for a trial period to start with.

Modesty pays

Because innovation is often viewed as a criticism of the old ways of doing things, commonsense dictates modesty in bringing in new ideas. 'I told you so,' will make people's hackles rise and they will secretly hope to see you fall flat on your face.

Don't make exaggerated claims in advance

Some of us are so keen to see a different method introduced that we oversell it, and when it doesn't achieve all that is expected of it, people regard it as a failure. So don't get carried away with your own enthusiasm and lead people to expect too much.

Involve people in the change

Use their experience and ingenuity by explaining the proposal and asking for their opinion. Then they will not be so likely to regard change as something alien, threatening their security, belittling them for being out of date. They will consider the change as partly their own, and take a proprietary interest in making it work. Next time somebody stands by and lets you make a fool of yourself when he could have given you a tip which would have averted the mistake, ask yourself why. Perhaps you could seek more help and not try to go it alone so much. And, of course, when the outcome is successful you have to see that all who helped get the credit.

Maintain the change

Because all changes have unforeseen side effects, it is important to appraise and maintain the new method. Don't forget to make the necessary adjustments, either to the system itself, or the surrounding circumstances.

What's in it for the staff?

Change is uncomfortable but profitable. It is perhaps unreasonable to expect those affected to have all the discomfort and none of the profit. In some cases the benefit is not a direct financial one. It may take the form of greater security because, by virtue of the change, the firm becomes more competitive and better able to retain its share of the trade. In other instances an immediate increase in productivity and profitability may result. If management waits for the union to fight for a share and then grudgingly yields, it will have to pay anyway, but in addition to the money it will pay in lost cooperation and goodwill. It is surely far better to say 'This is our saving. What share can we give our employees?'

In the short run, changes do sometimes affect people adversely and these harmful results must be guarded against. But in the past quarter of a century automation has given us all the chance of owning a refrigerator, a washing-machine, and a car. So change means a better life for everybody. Your responsibility as a supervisor is to help it along and try to make it painless.

Fig. 7.1. Checklist on introducing changes

Questions	× √	Notes
1. Do you explain the reasons for changes?		
2. Do you explain what benefits will be derived from any particular change?		
3. Do you tell everybody who will be affected?		
4. Do you tell them soon enough?		
5. Do you give them a chance to comment?		

Questions	$\times \sqrt{}$	Notes
6. Do you listen to their suggestions?		
7. If you have to reject a suggestion do you tell them why?		
8. Do you pass to your superior any significant comments?		
9. Do you consider whether this particular change will be better introduced gradually?		

10. Do you consider how it will affect:
    their self respect?
    their security?
    their sense of belonging to a team?		

11. Can you provide a way in which people can save face in accepting the change?		
12. Do you consider what support and assistance you can give to people to help them during the change?		
13. Are you patient and tolerant for those who will now find the going harder?		
14. Are you firm in your ultimate objectives?		
15. Are you prepared to make adjustments in your plans for getting there?		

Questions

1. Unrest is often caused by changes. If you were works manager, outline the steps you would take to introduce a major change in the operation of the factory.

2. Of what importance is effective communication when changes are being introduced at work?

3. How would you persuade an employee of the benefits of work study?

8. Reducing disciplinary problems

When people work in a company where the wages are good and where they have a pride in the end product and their part in producing it, where they have complete confidence in management and are adequately informed—under these conditions you do not often find that people break regulations. So the first essential for good order is to provide good leadership by following the guidelines which are given in chapters 1 and 2. Most people want to be able to carry on with the work in peace and are sensible enough to see that without rules and procedures to follow, without respect for supervisors, there would be anarchy. They themselves toe the line, and you owe it not only to yourself but to the law-abiders as well to see that the minority, too, behave in a responsible way.

Whether you find this easy or difficult depends partly on circumstances. Firstly the temptation to break regulations in the firm should, as far as possible, be removed. For example, in oil refineries the temptation to smoke in areas where it is forbidden is diminished by setting aside a special smoking area in which people are free to light up. Don't just accept a situation in which people are tempted to break a rule. Top management may not be aware of how unreasonable the rule is, so put up your recommendation on how it could be changed, giving your reasons. You may have to make the regulations impossible to break. If you are a parent you know that you not only have to tell young Albert not to move the hi fi . . . you fix it to the floor as well.

Second, it is more difficult to keep people in line when higher management takes away supervisors' authority by not keeping them informed of things that they should know, by not supporting them in action they take, by frequently reversing their decisions. or by giving orders directly to those under their control without reference to the supervisor in charge. If this happens to you, point out tactfully to your chief that it will make his job easier in the long run if he helps you by supporting you, informing you, and exerting managerial control through you, instead of bypassing your position and undermining your authority.

What the supervisor himself can do to reduce disciplinary problems

Set a good example. The way you do your job, how tidily you work, what time you arrive in the morning, the attitude you show towards management—these things have a strong influence on the attitudes of those under your control. If you privately think that some company regulations are unwise, or that a policy is wrong, tell your superior, but don't broadcast your disagreement to the staff. That will undermine their confidence in you and management.

Learn the rule book. Besides ensuring that you give people a fair deal, knowing the rule book will give you self-confidence.

Expect high standards. Recent research has shown that the best results are obtained by supervisors who expect the highest standards, thereby demonstrating confidence in people's ability and inclination to do a job well and to observe the rules in doing so. Leniency and tolerance of slack standards soon lead to discontent and the breakdown of discipline. Let everybody know that you expect the best they are capable of.

Give forewarnings. Occasionally regulations which have been allowed to lapse suddenly have to be re-established. When this occurs remember how useful it is to give a forewarning and a reason for tightening up. Legally you may be safe in taking action without doing so, but the employee affected will justifiably ask 'Why pick on me?'

Don't have favourites. Before you were a supervisor you could choose your friends and keep away from those you didn't want to bother with, but now you have to be available to all of them.

Find out what authority you have. If you have the responsibility for maintaining good order in your department you must have a certain amount of authority although you probably have to check with others before using some of it. It will make your job easier if you can find out exactly what powers have been granted to you. Try filling in the following analysis by putting a tick in the appropriate column of Fig. 8.1, If in doubt, ask your superior to give a ruling.

Fig. 8.1

Action	Complete authority	Check with somebody else before taking action
Manpower		
Decide to increase pay roll.		
Recruit replacements.		
Report on probationary employees.		
Transfer employees within your department.		
Arrange transfer with other departments.		
Lay people off for lack of work.		
Discipline		
Give written reprimand.		
Suspend from work.		
Discharge (very rare).		
Leadership		
Listen to grievances in the first instance.		
Accept written grievances from trade unions.		
Give written replies to these.		
Time off		
Grant leave of absence.		
Allow people to go home early in special circumstances.		
Training and education		
Carry out on-the-job training.		
Prepare apprentice-training rosters.		
Send people on courses.		

Fig. 8.1. (Contd)

Action	Complete authority	Check with some-body else before taking action
Arrange grants for company-sponsored studies.		
Safety		
Stop people working when there is a risk.		
Take unsafe tools and machinery out of service.		
Send employees for first aid.		
Make out accident reports.		
Services		
Requisition internal transport, lifting tackle, etc.		
Call on maintenance services.		
Call on electrical services.		
Quality		
Reject products.		
Be final judge on whether product will pass.		

Reprimands

The foregoing points dealt with keeping good order, and preventing acts of indiscipline. But if a reprimand *must* be given, how do you go about this? Here are some tips which will help you next time you have to reprimand. (Remember that your purpose is to prevent a recurrence and not to punish a culprit. If you can achieve this without applying sanctions so much the better.)

Don't turn a blind eye

If somebody comes in late, goes off early, works a machine without a guard or does anything else against the rules, don't turn a blind eye. By doing so, you are implying that it does not matter. Let him see that you have noticed and that you do not expect it to happen again. It is better to do this at the time, provided that by doing so you do not make him look small in front of others.

Don't act in anger

A spontaneous justified outburst does sometimes get results but it is usually dangerous to give way to this impulse. So often all the facts are not available and one is left looking a fool because the supposed culprit was in the right. Cool down, count ten, say you want to see him later—anything to give you time to deal calmly with the situation.

Prepare for the interview

If the problem is poor quality work, get the scrap figures or any error frequency records so that you can put the facts on the table. You will at least then both be starting on common ground with the same factual evidence to go on. Make time for the interview and hold it in private. If it is going to be a long session make sure the venue is also comfortable and quiet.

Plan your approach. What sort of a person is he, what is his wavelength? Will you start with a problem which you know is uppermost in his mind? If you haven't spoken to him for a long time perhaps you may have to re-establish contact first. One foreman in a machine shop wanted to caution his overhead crane operator for bad timekeeping, but had not communicated with him except by hand signals for seven years. Obviously there was some preparatory work to be done there. In most cases the sandwich method works well—that is, a kick in the pants in between two pats on the back.

Conduct the interview in two parts

Let him explain. You have put the problem to him, or commented on what you have observed. *Do not do this aggressively*, and do not judge too quickly or react too strongly at this stage. Take time to think. Draw out all the facts and feelings, including whether he has anything on his mind. At this stage your prime purpose is to ensure that you fully understand the situation.

When you have done this, you will probably want to verify the accuracy of what he has said, consult company policy, check the records, or talk it over with your boss. Then you can weigh and decide. Consider a range of alternatives at this point. Perhaps he needs training, a change of job, time to sort himself out, or a warning. Select the best alternative, but foresee the snags in pursuing it. For example, if you sack him, how is your depleted team going to meet that important deadline?

Advise him of your decision. If your company is unionized, your disciplinary procedure will probably require the presence of the union representative at this stage.

Figure 8.2 gives an example of the handling of a case in which a worker refused to operate a block and tackle over a chemical vat. The supervisor eventually found out that the fumes were causing respiratory troubles which the employee was reluctant to admit, and the remedy was a change of job.

Fig. 8.2

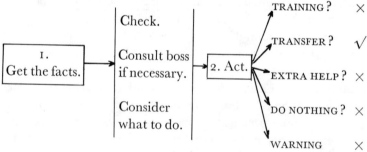

Written notes

If you have to leave a note in writing to convey what seems to you a very mild rebuke, think again. It is always better to communicate this kind of message face to face. The written word is so often misinterpreted unless explained and discussed.

Don't reprimand in front of others

If you do, you will belittle and arouse resentment.

Be careful when using wit

The humorous remark or witty observation is fine when there is a strong enough mutual understanding for it to be taken lightheartedly. The trouble is that witty criticisms can be taken as sarcasm and that invites rejoinders.

Use the 'law of the situation'

If you want to correct people you must appeal to their reason by telling them why they are expected to do whatever it is you are asking them to do. Instead of saying 'I'm telling you to do this', you say 'This is the situation, therefore this is what has to be done.' It is the situation which has laid down the law and not the supervisor. The appeal to a person's reason enables you to secure his cooperation and that applies whether he is your subordinate, colleague or even your boss.

Let the union know

Company policy varies on this point but many supervisors find it pays to tell the union representative what has happened (assuming you find out first!) and what you propose to do. Never ask him what action he suggests you take, of course—it is not his job to recommend punishment for his own constituents. Some supervisors like to have the union representative in attendance during the informal hearing of what the man has to say about the infraction. In most cases it seems good sense to keep the employee's representative in the picture, because it ensures that both he and management are working on the same set of facts and there is no distorting the truth about what happened and what was said.

Take his record into account

It is not favouritism simply to caution a worker who, for the first time in a year, works the machine without a guard—nor is it victimization to suspend a man who does the same thing but who has a long history of unsafe practices and has been involved in one or two accidents.

Consider suspension without pay

There are two situations in which this can be used. The first is as an interim measure with the object of removing from the workplace an employee who, through his presumed fault, is temporarily not in a fit state to do his job, such as being intoxicated or involved in a brawl. In this case he would be required to go home for the rest of the shift and report next day when appropriate action would be taken.

The other situation is when it is decided to impose suspension as a penalty. This measure should only be used if the employee's contract of employment provides for it, or if it is accepted by custom and practice. It should only be taken with the approval of the person in your organization who is responsible for industrial relations. The trade union will sometimes accept it as a preferable alternative to dismissal.

Know and use the company's disciplinary procedure

Many companies have drawn up a disciplinary procedure, and if there is a union it will almost certainly have been agreed with them. It is important that you should find out if such a procedure exists in your own organization, and that you should know and observe it, because failure to do so would undermine your position. Procedures of this kind normally operate as follows:

1. The first step is a verbal warning or, in the case of more serious misconduct, a written warning setting out the circumstances.
2. No employee should be dismissed for a first breach of discipline except in the case of gross misconduct.
3. Action on any further misconduct, for example, final warning, suspension or dismissal, should be recorded in writing.
4. Details of disciplinary action should be given in writing to the employee and, if he so wishes, to his employee representative.
5. No disciplinary action should be taken against a shop steward until the circumstances of the case have been discussed with a full-time official of the union concerned.

Good discipline is a matter of adjustment

Obviously the best discipline is to be found in a department where reprimands are unnecessary, and your aim must always be to achieve that state of affairs.

Fig. 8.3. Checklist on good order

Questions	X √	Notes
1. Are company regulations observed in your department?		
2. Do employees avoid wasting their time or others' time?		
3. Are instructions promptly and willingly carried out?		
4. Do they do a good day's work, even in your absence?		
5. Do they set a good example to other departments, e.g., not stopping their work by chatter, etc.?		
6. Do you know all your people individually?		
7. Are you fair in your treatment of staff?		
8. Do you treat them with due consideration for their self-respect?		
9. Do you get people to use self-discipline?		
10. Is there any pilfering?		
11. Do staff take undue advantage of normal breaks?		
12. Is there cleanliness and good house-keeping?		
13. Do you set a good example?		
14. Do you know the extent and limits of your authority in suspending or dismissing?		
15. Do you avoid undermining your subordinates?		
16. Do your subordinates respect your position and not by-pass you to the boss?		
17. Do you avoid implying 'It's the boss's order, not mine'?		
18. Do you give instructions clearly and confidently?		
19. Do your people observe the safety regulations?		

Questions	×√	Notes
20. Is there a low accident rate?		
21. Is there a good industrial relationship with the union representative?		
22. Do you know the company's disciplinary procedure?		
23. Do you know employer—employee law as it affects you?		

Questions

1. How would you reprimand an employee for careless and poor quality work?

2. How can the supervisor obtain good discipline in his team?

3. One of your staff is continually going to your manager with small complaints even though you have asked him to come to you first. How can you deal with this situation?

4. An employee often leaves his workplace and spends long periods in the cloakroom. What would you do about this? What would you do if your first line of action produced little improvement?

9. *Your responsibility for communication*

The Sauropoda Dinosaur had communication problems. It was possible for a mesozoic midge to raise lumps on his tail that had practically gone septic by the time the news reached the brain. So another brain was installed half way along. Its job was to help out with communication by relaying messages and generally looking after the flow of information to and from the limbs under its control.

Communication is an important part of the supervisor's job in industry. In the very early stages of the development of a business the owner could deal directly with his staff, telling them about its competitive position and the effects of demand and markets upon it. In return, he would be personally interested in them as individuals, knowing and making allowances for them and their problems, limitations, and special aptitudes.

Later would come the dinosaur stage—the business would grow, the owner become removed from the staff owing to his other management and business preoccupations, and a supervisor would take his place in each department. Eventually two or three more levels of management would come between him and the supervisor, and by then it would be important to do something to maintain communication.

The owner of the business would still try to do his rounds as often as possible but would be forced to delegate the personal contact and exchange of opinions, feelings and information to his representative, the supervisor.

Some supervisors look at the elaborate communication network in their companies. They see:

Dinosaur Ltd

the company magazine
the bulletin
the noticeboard
the loudspeaker system

and they wash their hands of all responsibility for passing and
receiving information: 'I don't need to bother now—top
management is communicating direct.' They forget that you

cannot *discuss* with a magazine, bulletin or noticeboard and that you can read the wrong message between the lines. All these are only aids to communication. They are better than no communication at all but they are not personal enough. There is no opportunity for question and answer, and you cannot see the expression on the other fellow's face.

As supervisor, you should be the direct personal link between the staff and top management. You have a clear responsibility to communicate downwards, and upwards to your superior.

Communicating downwards

You must interpret management's policy decisions and actions favourably to your staff. If you disagree with them you may say so to the management, but your disagreement is not for publication and you are bound to support your employer in public.

You should obtain and pass on enough information about the job, the department and the company to enable your people to work intelligently and with the enthusiasm which comes of knowing what it is all for. If senior management does not volunteer much information, don't wait to be told: ask.

There are five main methods of keeping your staff in the picture:

1. Make sure that new staff receive a proper briefing when you induct them into the department.
2. Ensure that they know their terms of reference and targets and their progress in achieving them.
3. Make a point of having daily contact with every member of your staff in order to:

    ▷ set standards (tidiness, safety, personal appearance, punctuality, conduct, etc.)
    ▷ show appreciation,
    ▷ give constructive criticism or guidance where needed,
    ▷ ask if there are questions or problems and sort them out.

4. Call the occasional staff meeting to pass on information you

may have received from your superior, explain plans and impending changes, or review past performance as a basis for your future intentions.

5. Ensure that the notice board in your department is up to date, tidy and a good testimony of the importance you place on communication.

Communicating upwards

Your chief is interested in two main items, the *staff* and the *work*.

The staff

It is true that joint consultative committees have an important part to play in keeping top management in touch with the staff's opinions and ideas, but so has the supervisor.

1. You should keep your chief informed about people's problems, feelings, reactions and ideas.
2. Besides being management's advocate to them you should be their advocate to management. In companies where section leaders leave all this to the union, the shop stewards and full-time officials spend too much of their time making up for management's own poor communication. It is understandable if from there they go on to start trying to run the business.

The work

What should you tell your superior about the work and its progress? He needs enough information about what you are doing to ensure that he will never be taken by surprise by his own boss or by another department concerning duties and responsibilities which have been allocated to you. For example he would look pretty incompetent if, in the dining room, another department head commented, 'I see you had a nasty accident in "B" Machine shop this morning'—and he knew nothing about it. Here are the main classifications of information he needs from you:

Progress on long-term work. Periodic reports from you, monthly or quarterly, should keep him briefed on how any major project is developing. Perhaps the project involves the planned standard-ization of equipment by means of specified replacements to worn-out non-standard machinery, or it may be the long-term training of your staff to make the section more flexible. He needs to have an up-to-date mental picture of how such jobs are going along.

He needs to know about exceptional events. You can overdo progress reporting. It would be time-wasting for everybody to report frequently that everything is normal. So we use the 'management by exception' principle, which means that you only report when there is something significant to say. The next four classifications are examples of significant events which would warrant informing him.

Completion of assignment. Suppose the filing system has had to be reorganized and old documents separated off into the dead file store. He will expect to be told when you have done the job.

Anticipated problems. You are often better able to foresee problems than he is, so make sure that he is warned in time to take action.

You can often foresee problems more easily than the boss

Deviation from plan. The job is scheduled for completion on 1 May, but you are behind because two of the staff have been away sick and one of your suppliers was late with a delivery. It is important to let the boss know this so that he can take steps to speed the job up further along the line, warn the customer, and perhaps call in outside help. So he relies on you to tell him the facts, however unpleasant.

Suggestions about work method changes. These may come from you or your subordinate. Remember to give credit to whoever thought up the bright idea, and try to *sell* it if it is a good one. Choose the right time to broach the subject, when he is not too busy, and support the idea with facts and figures. If possible put it down on paper. It strengthens your case if you can show savings over a period of months. It is not enough to put up your ideas and leave the boss to do all the spadework on them. Think through the snags and find the answers to his possible objections so that the idea does not have to be shelved pending further information.

It will pay to let the matter rest if you are getting nowhere. The seed of your idea may develop and bear fruit later. Provided he does not forget whose idea it was, the delay does no harm.

Fig. 9.1. Checklist on communication

Questions	× √	Notes
1. Is there evidence of an interchange of ideas between you and other supervisors?		
2. Is there a smooth flow of work from your department or section and those on either side of it?		
3. Do you consult the specialists in the organization?		
4. Do you know who to go to with your questions or those raised by the staff?		
5. Do you have a clear understanding of the borderline between your responsibilities and others?		
6. Do you maintain a good working relationship with colleagues?		
7. Do you know all of your subordinates by name?		
8. Do they all clearly know who their boss is?		
9. Do you know who yours is? Do you sometimes feel you have two bosses?		
10. Do your employees know the reasons for the jobs which they are asked to do? Are they not simply being told: 'because the superintendent says so'.		
11. Are you able to introduce changes in your work group without major upsets?		
12. Do you manage to deal with problems, and so avoid their being brought up through the union?		
13. Do you take up ideas put forward by the staff and secure action on them or explain why they cannot be acted upon?		
14. Do you consult those nearest the job on matters affecting the work?		

Questions	× √	Notes
15. Do you take your subordinate supervisors into your confidence?		
16. Are you careful about the introduction of new employees to see that they quickly become members of the working team?		
17. Do all your subordinates know what their jobs are?		
18. Are there no dangerous rumours in circulation?		
19. Do your subordinate supervisors seldom get bypassed in the flow of information?		
20. Do you?		
21. Do you take up, on subordinates' behalf, questions which they have raised with you but which you cannot answer?		
22. Do your employees show a sustained interest in their jobs?		
23. Does the department function smoothly without staff constantly coming to you for information which they ought to have been given?		
24. Do you often go round your department (once a day at least)?		
25. Are you available enough?		

Questions

1. Give your views on joint consultation.
2. How is morale affected by the standard of communication within the organization?
3. How can management ensure that there is a full interchange of information at all levels?
4. Why is good communication so important in a company?
5. Is the grapevine an advantage to a company? Please give reasons.

10. *The supervisor's responsibility for safety*

Every supervisor must concern himself with the safety of his staff for three main reasons:

The humanitarian reason. This is the straightforward responsibility to one's fellowmen for their safety. The social conscience of industry has developed considerably over the past 50 years. The Forth rail bridge completed in 1890 cost 57 lives. The road bridge, no less impressive, completed in 1964 cost three, but we must never be complacent. A bridge is not, in humanitarian terms, worth one man's death, and the same concern for human life must extend to all industrial activity.

The legal responsibility. The law makes it obligatory for a company to provide safe working conditions and insists on the use of safe working methods. Cases are on record of supervisors themselves being fined for contravening the law in this respect.

The economic reason. Accidents cost very much more than the cheques for compensation and fines. Often there is material damage, as in the case of a factory fire. Then there is the cost of lost work, which is often increased by failure to meet production deadlines and, possibly, by the loss of customer goodwill. There is the loss of time in the investigation of the accident, and in people giving evidence, or talking about it, spoilt material and damaged tools. There are many hidden losses too; a shop where there are accidents is not a happy workplace, and low morale will always affect people's job-enthusiasm and therefore their productivity. The economic reason alone is a powerful enough one to justify every effort to keep down accidents.

Many firms have a safety officer, and supervisors sometimes make the mistake of thinking that safety is really *his* business, not theirs. In fact, of course, it is *everybody's* business, but the man who can do most to prevent accidents is the supervisor himself. In one large firm, 3000 employees and 600 supervisors co-operated in a survey to find out what factors contributed most to safety in their company and they listed the following points in this order:

1. Employees' safety attitude.
2. Training and instruction.
3. Provision of safe tools and equipment.
4. Supervision and leadership.
5. Management's safety attitude.
6. Safe methods and working practices.
7. Warning signs and signals.
8. First-aid training.
9. Love of home and family.
10. Presence of supervisor.
11. Safety meetings.
12. Tool inspections.
13. Safety films.

The significant thing about this list is that all of the top four items and most of the remainder are directly influenced by the supervisor himself.

The safety department's task is to help managers and supervisors in their job of getting the work done safely. They give advice, keep meaningful statistics on accidents for management's and supervisors' guidance, lend their weight to pressure for safer working conditions, and provide accident prevention aids like non-slip stickers, reflectors, guards, and safety posters.

The safety officer normally has no more authority on the shopfloor than one manager has in another's department. He is not usually given authority to hold up production and tell a man to do the job in another way, any more than a supervisor can in somebody else's department. He would preferably contact the man's superior at the earliest possible moment and tell him

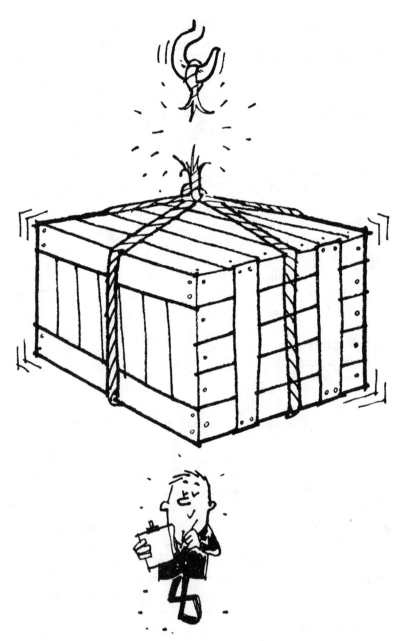

Make a point of checking on safety matters

what he had seen. In an emergency, of course, commonsense should prevail. Anyone seen smoking in an oil refinery could rightly be reprimanded immediately by anybody in authority. or by any fellow-worker, for that matter.

It is logical that you cannot normally have safety officers crossing the lines of authority, issuing orders and reprimands, and equally logical that they cannot be held responsible for the individual unsafe acts of all workers. The supervisors have this responsibility and the safety officer helps them to fulfil it.

How can you promote safety in your department?

Set a good example

Actions speak louder than words. It is important that you show in everything you do that your motto is 'Safety First'. Remember that, even though you are 100 per cent sure you could do something unsafe and get away with it, you must refrain from doing so because of the bad example you will be setting to others.

In your inspection tours, make a point of checking on safety matters

Look at the checklists at the end of this chapter to remind yourself of some of the things to look for. Write in other points that matter in your job.

Be insistent towards management about points of safety

One works manager told a group of managers and foremen at a conference that they must make a nuisance of themselves in his office if they ever thought a safety point was being overlooked in spite of repeated reminders. Managers have to respond to pressures from customers and superiors to get production out. They cannot do their job properly unless people below them have the courage to put with equal insistence the need for safe practices.

Insist that people do things the safe way

It may sound like nagging, and you may be reluctant to make a nuisance of yourself, but remember that every man will respect you more for your interest in his safety.

Investigate accidents to prevent recurrences

Find out who and what caused the accident. Don't make the mistake of thinking that accidents 'just happen'. Every accident is caused by something which somebody does, or fails to do. Track down the cause and ensure that it will never happen again.

Provide protective clothing

Protective clothing does not stop the accident happening but it does minimize the injury. Just by putting on his goggles a grindstone operator does not prevent himself from having an accident. To do that he must be sure that the stone is not cracked, that it is being run at the right number of revs, and used for the right purpose. But protective clothing is a safeguard. If an accident is caused by some human failing somewhere, its effects are minimized by the protection given.

Remember the special problems of your older workers

Taking this to mean people over 55, there are certain factors which must be considered in assigning work to them. Age may bring wisdom but it does not always bring sufficient self-knowledge for a man to know what he can, and can no longer do.

Many older staff have quicker wits than people half their age, but on the whole they tend to have slower reactions, a less ready grasp of new work techniques, and less accurate sight and hearing. Some may have a tendency to dizziness or drowsiness, and a greater tendency to falling and a greater susceptibility to injury when doing so.

These factors should not deter you from employing or continuing to employ older men and women. Often their experience and proven loyalty more than outweigh the drawbacks, but the shortcomings must be reckoned with in spite of the fact that many people conceal their disabilities because they are afraid of the consequences of complaining. Here are some safety tips for dealing with older people on the job:

1. See that the lighting is adequate and provide extra if necessary.
2. Give them less arduous work.

3. Provide seats, if possible.
4. Observe their particular weak points, and avoid placing them in jobs in which their handicaps could be a danger to themselves or others.

(Please turn to chapter 16 for further advice on the supervision of older employees.)

Youngsters have problems too

Newcomers to industry have their own problems of adjustment. They are probably unused to the hazards of the shopfloor, with heavy, noisy dangerous machinery. They are usually inexperienced at the job, anxious not to appear timid, unaccustomed to the monotony of some types of work which requires close attention, and perhaps inclined to high spirits and horseplay.

The accident prone

Safety records show that accidents happen more frequently to a small number of employees and that most never have any at all. The few who are most frequently involved are known as 'accident prone'. Often their susceptibility to accidents is the result of inadequate training or high work pressure. Perhaps the working environment is particularly dangerous. A few accident-prone people are inclined that way because of some psychological state—something in their character which makes them try to evade the rules, buck the system, not only on the job but in everything they do. It may be something which gives them a tendency to self-injury or self-destruction; perhaps just a lackadaisical attitude to life in general.

Accident-prone people must be identified, and, in the first instance, drilled in safe ways of working. The ultimate resort—a change of jobs—may have to be faced in extreme cases which do not respond to other remedies.

Accident-prone people must be identified

Run your own safety meetings

When some potential source of accident becomes apparent, it is a good idea to call the group together round a machine, outline the problem and ask for suggestions. There may be no specific hazard but you may wish to have a general discussion about safety to bring the matter to the forefront of their minds. By asking for their suggestions you enlist their support for your safety objectives without thereby losing any of your authority, because the last word is always with you.

Run your own safety meeting

Your union representative will be glad to lend his support, for in the matter of safety your objectives and his are the same. Quite apart from its value as an accident prevention measure, this will very probably pave the way for greater cooperation and understanding on other issues too.

How safety-minded are you?

Figure 10.1 gives a checklist which you can use to improve your own standards.

Fig. 10.1. Checklist on safety

Work methods and training

1. Do you ensure that unskilled staff in your section do not practise using dangerous machinery without expert guidance?
2. Are the right tools provided?
3. Do you ensure that they are kept in good condition?

4. Are the appropriate people assigned to potentially dangerous jobs?
5. Do you ensure that staff do not take unsafe short cuts?

6. Are machines fitted with the necessary guards?
7. Do you ensure that guards are used?
8. Are machines switched off when not in use?
9. Does your department *condition* people to safety?
10. Do your staff show safety-consciousness?
11. Are they well informed about potential hazards?
12. Do you stress safety during the induction of new staff?

13. Are newcomers alerted to local dangers?

14. Do you ensure correct handling and lifting methods are used?
15. Have those staff who have to lift heavy or awkward loads received training in manual lifting and handling?
16. Are there proper emergency drills and are these known?
17. Do you arrange refresher safety training?
18. Do you ensure that your people are trained to use the correct signals?

19. Do you ever give your staff pep talks on safety?
20. Is there a planned maintenance programme?
21. Is maintenance safely carried out in your opinion?
22. Are adequate isolation switches used?
23. Do you ensure that correct methods are used in slinging loads?
24. Would you stop production to make something safe?
25. Are the guards on your machines in good working order?

26. Have you considered painting the guards in a conspicuous colour?
27. Do you thoroughly know your plant?
28. In planning a job, do you make the safety angle an important part of your plan, anticipating dangers?
29. Have you ever arranged a safety competition for your staff?

30. Do you ensure that you have enough help for a dangerous job?
31. Do you and your staff know the safety regulations and the reasons behind them?

32. Are you strict about safety?
33. Do you arrange for automatic safety devices to be fitted when possible?

34. Do you try to avoid distractions?

Fire

1. Do you know and observe the fire regulations? Does everybody in your department?
2. Do you have the extinguishers you need?
3. Have you recently held a fire practice?
4. Is there an adequate alarm system?

5. Is your fire-fighting equipment regularly tested?

6. Are you strict about smoking only in prescribed areas?
7. Are these clearly defined?
8. Do you know the fire exits and are they kept clear?
9. Do you and your people know how to use the extinguishers?
10. Are the fire doors kept free at all times and closed when the factory is empty?
11. In the event of fire could you be sure that everybody was out of the building?

Electrical dangers

1. Are electrical installations safe, especially temporary ones?
2. Are all points, A C and D C, clearly marked?
3. Are power tools working off a low voltage with a transformer?
4. Do you avoid the misuse of electrical equipment?
5. Do you know where the main switches are?
6. Is a competent person nominated for electrical maintenance in the department?

First aid

1. Do you insist on prompt first aid for injuries?
2. Do you have a trained 'first aider' and have you and he access to an adequate first-aid box?
3. Do the staff know where to go if first aid is needed?

General

1. Do you practise what you preach about safety?
2. Do you consider your own health and safety?
3. Is there good discipline (absence of horseplay)?
4. Is there adequate protective clothing?
5. Do you see that people use it?

6. Do you encourage people to report hazards?
7. Do you act promptly on these reports?
8. Do you investigate accidents to prevent recurrences?
9. Do you arrange an adequate follow-up on this?
10. Do you know and observe any legal requirements concerning the materials and machines you supervise?
11. Has your department a good safety record?
12. Do you continually consider what you can do to improve it?

13. Do you have proper storage facilities for dangerous materials?
14. Have you adequate safety posters?
15. Is there a clearly defined place for safety equipment?
16. Are barrier creams supplied where necessary
17. Do you encourage safety suggestions and is there a recognized channel for these?
18. Do you avoid dangerously long hours?
19. Do you guard against fatigue risks?
20. Do you guard against stress endangering any employee?
21. Do employees know whom they must contact at all times in case of an accident?

22. Is there adequate protective clothing, and does *everybody*, including visitors, use it?
23. Do you report accident statistics to the staff?

24. Are there clear markings to identify the correct stacking areas?
25. Are stacks safe?
26. Has the layout of your workplace been planned with safety in mind?
27. Is there adequate space between machines?
28. Do you arrange an adequate check-up after installation?
29. Are steam pipes safely covered?
30. Are compressed air or pressure vessels regularly tested?
31. Have you arranged for safety glass to be fitted where advisable?
32. Are poisonous materials properly supervised?
33. Are pipes correctly colour-coded?
34. Are accidents publicized to prevent recurrences?
35. Do you know the safety laws as they affect you?
36. Do you ensure unauthorized entry is prevented?
37. Is there emergency lighting?
38. Are there adequate warning signals?
39. Have you an easy reference for the telephone numbers of the fire brigade and the medical department or doctor?
40. Do you consult your union representative on safety?
41. Do you insist on rules about no running?
42. Do the emergency stop buttons work properly?

Inspection

1. Do you keep your eyes open for hazards?
2. Is the workplace tidy?
3. Is the lighting adequate?
4. Are the gangways and exits kept clear?

5. Are hazards eliminated or clearly marked?
6. Are the floors safe (e.g. no slippery substances on floor, ruts eliminated, pits properly covered)?

7. If you use footboards are they in a safe condition?

8. Do you ensure that transport and lifting tackle are safe?

9. Do you ask to see the Factory Inspectors' reports?

10. Are openings roped off or otherwise safeguarded?

11. Are the safety regulations displayed?

12. Are staff safely dressed?

13. Are safe working loads observed?

14. Are there safe ladders and staging?

Never remove the guard from your machine

Questions

1. Give the outline of a safety talk which you would deliver to your staff at the start of Safety Week in your organization.

2. Annual reports of the Chief Inspector of Factories show that approximately 20 per cent of all accidents are caused by incorrect handling and lifting of goods. You are the safety officer of an engineering factory. Your directors have noticed the latest reports and have asked you to outline the steps that you propose taking to ensure that such accidents are reduced to the lowest possible figure. Draft your proposals in a report.

3. You are walking through a department which is not your own and you see an employee doing his job with the safety guard off his machine. What can you do?

4. As a supervisor how can you foster safety-consciousness among staff and enlist their cooperation in reducing accidents?

5. 'Safety is the Safety Officer's job.' Why is this statement misleading and potentially dangerous?

6. What would you do if an employee were negligent about wearing eye protection? What would be your next step if he took little notice?

7. What would you do if an employee had a spate of accidents?

11. *Your shop steward and you*

Trade unions have an important and constructive part to play in industry. Although management and employees have a common purpose in their work, there will always be a degree of contention about how to divide the income, and about injustices, real or imagined, which arise in the process of earning it.

Unions can be a help to management if they are directed towards an ideal of responsible industrial citizenship, and this is more likely to happen if management accepts their role in a positive way and does everything possible to encourage an open and mutually confident approach.

Properly established and recognized, a trade union can help management in the following ways:

1. It can provide management with a coherent and unified workforce with which to negotiate.
2. It can reassure employees that justice has been done, by supporting mutually agreed compromises.
3. It can ventilate and express grievances which might otherwise fester away unnoticed and ultimately induce paralysis, because discontented staff do not work efficiently.
4. It can build morale.

Your relationship with your shop steward

There are about 200 000 shop stewards in British industry. The majority of them are dedicated people doing a difficult and often thankless job without any reward except the satisfaction of being of service. The union representative is in an awkward position. He is paid by management, to whom he sometimes

Your shop steward has a tricky job

looks like a deliberate agitator; elected by the staff, who some-times suspect him of being a management stooge, and he is under the vigilance of the trade union, with whose rules he is expected to conform even when they apparently oppose the men's short-term needs. He has to safeguard each member's individual interests, while preserving the trade union legacy of which he is the main custodian. Yet he must help to preserve the company's prosperity which alone can guarantee that of the men who elected him. He spends on average eleven hours a week of company time on union business and five hours of his own leisure time. His authority depends on the confidence he can win and maintain amongst the union's rank and file members, and he can only survive if he has a strong character, calmness and plenty of commonsense.

He is now assuming more significance on the industrial scene and his power will grow with the importance of local wage negotiations and the tendency for trade union branch life to be increasingly based on the workplace.

Companies who are faced with many different unions and wish to take prompt action in an emergency are often glad to deal with shop stewards rather than have the matter referred back to district or national level. So they, too, make his job important.

How should the supervisor deal with the problems of super-vision and communication which are caused by this shift in the distribution of trade union power?

Don't use him as your mouthpiece

It is a mistake to use the shop steward as *your spokesman* in conveying messages to your employees, whether these are purely informational, or whether they are warnings about lateness or other infractions. It is not his job to communicate on manage-ment's behalf. He is there to protect the men's interests and he cannot put across to them with enthusiasm or conviction policies or instructions with which he may later have to disagree. Management must do its own communicating and the logical way of going about this is to tell the supervisor and let him pass it on to all of his subordinates.

Keep him informed

If he knows what is going on and what your plans are he can calm down members who come to him with exaggerated rumours and suspicions.

Consult him

Try not to react defensively when your staff offer an opinion, or to say, or think 'Are they trying to tell me how to do my job?'

It is no reflection on your leadership if you consult them or the shop steward when you propose taking action on a matter which affects their interests. If you are going to make changes or take an unusual course of action you will find it much easier with prior consultation. You still have the last word, but they will appreciate having been asked their views.

Courtesy always pays

I have asked over 200 shop stewards the question: 'What advice would you give to supervisors on their dealings with you?' They always say, 'Tell them courtesy pays.' It costs nothing to call someone by his name and to give him your undivided attention for a few minutes a day. Remember he is the focal point through which many of the section's grievances pass. Don't regard him as a difficult individual, but as the man who happens to be holding a particularly difficult office.

One transport department supervisor used to talk over cases with his shop steward in the presence of his chargehand and a clerk, and consequently felt he always had to put on an act and assert his authority. The shop steward said that if he could catch him in the yard and go and sit with him in the quiet of one of the driving cabs, he became quite a different man—reasonable, calm, and prepared to admit he might be wrong. Everybody always has to act slightly differently when a third person is present, so if you think an audience could spoil your interview, conduct it in private. Ask the clerk to look after the telephone. Sometimes in a tense situation you will need to have someone present as a witness, and if he has one, so should you but it should be possible to have off the record communication as well.

If you have to give a severe reprimand, try to have the shop steward there

It is natural enough for anybody who is smarting under a reprimand to present a biased account when he tells his story to his representative. Often the shop steward finds himself with conflicting stories about what happened—the supervisor says one thing and the man another. If you have the shop steward present when you issue your warning you will find that he is in a much better position to deal fairly with the case, and will not be deceived by an incomplete account of the facts.

Learn the procedure and observe it

If you break with procedure you will weaken any case which may arise and unnecessarily damage your relationship with the representative.

Learn the rules and observe them

Unless you do you will create problems for yourself and the shop steward who probably has at least one barrack-room lawyer among his constituents.

Have a good working knowledge of employer–employee law

Don't leave him to handle all complaints and grievances

If you regard him as unofficial welfare officer in the department you may lose personal contact with your team. Encourage individuals to come straight to you with their grievances. He is there to give support to an individual only if the supervisor is unable to give an answer which satisfies the person concerned.

Don't delegate the compiling of rotas (e.g., overtime, shiftwork, holidays) to him

This is part of supervision, and needs to be done with a sound knowledge of job requirements. Moreover, if an employee is dissatisfied with the rota and his shop steward is the one who organized it, he has nobody else to whom he can appeal.

Try to see ways round restrictive practices

Restrictive practices are arrangements which were originally meant to protect people's jobs and levels of income. But today they do not always make sense, and can result in overmanning, wasteful job demarcations, unnecessary overtime and sheer boredom and frustration, all of which put up costs and sap enthusiasm. When this happens it is a direct threat to the security of the company and everyone employed there. The shop stewards have little choice but to abide by the rules, and it is no good trying to force them to abandon this kind of custom. When you see such practices impeding efficiency, sound out the shop steward's views, and then try to suggest to your superior ways in which the work could be carried out more logically. This could be just the kind of bargaining point which the company is looking for in the next round of negotiations.

Know the union

If you know the union rules, its structure, who has the power, and when officials are due to come up for re-election, you will understand the attitudes of the people you are dealing with. For example, an official whose term of office is expiring and who wants to be re-elected, can be an uncompromising bargainer. So it will probably pay the company to postpone any negotiations which are due until after the voting.

Conclusion

Your shop steward must play his part in representing the employees of the company, just as the buyer represents the market, and the board of directors represents the shareholders. In order to negotiate in an enlightened way and to do his job with a sense of responsibility, he needs *recognition* and *information*. You can play your part in seeing that he receives both, and can appreciate why management sometimes unintentionally makes the mistake of giving more of these two commodities to him than to you.

Fig. 11.1. Checklist on working with your union representative

Questions	$\times$ $\sqrt{}$	Notes
1. Do you avoid asking him to make announcements to the men on your behalf?		
2. Do you keep him informed of your intentions?		
3. Are you good at passing on to him those items of information which top management wish you to?		
4. Do you consult him on matters concerning the staff?		
5. Do you treat him as courteously as you would a fellow supervisor?		
6. Do you consider whether to have him in attendance when you issue a reprimand?		
7. Do you know and observe the procedure?		
8. Do you know and observe the rules and agreements?		
9. Do you know your company's policy on union membership		
10. Do you know your company's policy on allowing the union representative to deal with union business during working hours?		
11. Do you know and use the agreed grievance procedure and disciplinary procedure?		
12. Do you know whether you have the authority to reprimand, suspend, or dismiss?		
13. Does your union representative know and adhere to grievance procedure?		
14. Have you read the Code of Industrial Relations Practice?		
15. Do you know employer–employee law sufficiently well to keep out of trouble?		

Questions

1. How can the supervisor and union representative best work together for the good of the company and the employees of the department?

2. It is said that management gets the sort of shop steward it deserves. Discuss this statement.

12. *Don't do it all yourself*

Are you a supervisor or a superworker? The supervisor's job is to plan, organize, coordinate the work within his department and his department's work with the rest of the organization, give instructions and ensure that output is being maintained according to plan. Like the captain of a ship he should be in overall control. Nobody is going to be impressed if the skipper is setting a good example in the galley or engine room and neglecting his own job.

Who's on the bridge?

The most effective managers and supervisors are those who spend their time doing accurately and effectively the task which only they can do, not everybody else's work. Yet you will hear them say, 'I could do it more quickly myself than if I stop to explain.' 'We are short-handed. I have to let some of my jobs go by the board while I give a hand on production.' This seems an easy way out. Production usually does not need so much thought as supervision, and it is sometimes a sign of subconsciously dodging the real job.

It is also a shortsighted view. If you take the trouble to explain the job, others will know how to do it next time. If you are understaffed, could it be that people are leaving because they aren't receiving proper supervision? The supervisor could spend his time better by making a case to management for one extra employee.

In a stone quarry one of the more difficult and dangerous (but fortunately infrequent) jobs consists of lowering yourself commando fashion on a rope down the quarry face and dislodging dangerous outcrops. One quarry manager used to do this himself, probably as a kind of ritual. But what does it prove? Will he have to retire when he can no longer do it? Obviously not, since his organizing and leadership ability can outlast his physical prowess. Such activities have been called 'occupational hobbies'. Be careful not to indulge yourself for more than five per cent of the time on yours.

Delegating duties

Many supervisors find that they can go further than simply keeping their hands off the work which their staff ought to handle—they can actively delegate. This means giving somebody below you a job which you used to do yourself, or would have done yourself, and allowing him to finish it without hindrance. This is not always easy and you obviously cannot go against trade union regulations or overload somebody who already has too much work. But there is more scope for delegating than most people think. When you let subordinates make *decisions* you relieve yourself of the thinking (though not of the responsibility), eliminate delays while they wait for your answers, and develop their capabilities and powers of judgement. Most welcome the chance of using more discretion in their jobs and the increased self-confidence, understanding and experience they gain. Some may ask for more money if a great deal of work is delegated; if they deserve it, and it is feasible, why not? It may pay to have fewer, more capable staff with higher wages than twice as many people who cannot do much without their supervisor's help.

What duties can you start delegating? Write down every-thing you have to do in the course of your work. Do not put in too much detail. Follow the kind of plan shown in Fig. 12.1.

Fig. 12.1. Work delegation plan

What I do	Who can do it now?	Who could do it when trained?
Allocate jobs to sections in conjunction with section heads.	—	—
Check samples for quality.	All section supervisors.	
Order materials for whole department.	—	J. Clifford, section supervisor.
Recommend salary adjustments.	All section supervisors.	
Show Safety Inspector around department.	L. Rogers, section supervisor.	
Call in service department in case of breakdown.	All section supervisors.	
Plan departmental training programme for apprentices.		Section supervisors.

There should be three columns in all. The first is headed 'What I do', the second, 'Who can do it now?', and the third, 'Who could do it when trained?' When you systematically consider how to pass these duties down the line you may be able to offload a quarter of your day-to-day worries immediately. Others can be allocated when the people you think could be trained to help you are ready to do so. You will probably need to let your superior know of your delegation plans and obtain his approval, and he, of course, will make it clear that the responsibility still remains yours.

Begin by delegating duties which recur. Usually they are routine, not too difficult, and because of their frequency, take up most time. Then you can probably delegate those items which you personally are least qualified to handle if you have an employee who is something of an expert. There is no disgrace in one of your men being able to do a job better than you. The higher one is promoted, the more this is likely to be the case.

Some kinds of job can be delegated mainly as a means of training. Ask yourself:

▷ What kind of experience do I want to give this person in order to develop his full value to the enterprise?
▷ What could I delegate that is related to the jobs he is already doing?
▷ What duties can I delegate which have a satisfying and evident result when properly completed?
▷ What duties can I delegate to particular people in view of their special aptitudes and inclinations, thereby ensuring that they will be carried through willingly?
▷ What can I delegate which will give people the right amount of challenge?
▷ What sequence of delegations can I arrange so that each of my staff achieves a series of successes?

Here are some useful tips to help you in carrying through your programme of delegation.

Delegate the thinking and decision making as well as the doing. You are not delegating unless you leave sufficient discretionary powers to the man who has to do the job. In the best-run firms, from the managing director downwards, every decision is taken at the lowest possible level. The policy that underlies all decisions is formulated at the top and communicated downwards so that everybody knows what it is and why it is so.

Delegate the right to be wrong. Any work decision is based on knowledge and experience which will produce two or three alternative solutions to the problem in hand. The final decision is a matter of discretion—often a question of weighing each alternative and selecting the best. If the person to whom you have delegated the job has enough knowledge and experience, but in weighing the alternatives he makes a different choice from yours, resist the temptation to interfere. His decision may turn out to be wrong—but he has to have the right to make it. If he doesn't, he will form the habit of checking back constantly and relying too heavily on your advice.

Stand by his decisions and accept responsibility for them. Supervision is a tough job. It looks as though your subordinate will get the credit if the project turns out well and you will be blamed if it fails. Some supervisors keep a card on their desk inscribed 'The buck stops here'. There is no doubt that every supervisor and manager is responsible for the actions of his subordinates and it could not be otherwise, but managers do not usually overlook the fact that good results from the team mean good supervision. If one of your staff makes a mistake, stand by him and his reasons for making it, even if the decision itself cannot be justified, and accept overall responsibility. He will save face if you let him rectify his own error instead of stepping in yourself.

Tie in training with delegation. You learn from your mistakes, of course, but too many errors can be demoralizing. So try and explain to your subordinate before you delegate. Once he has mastered the essentials, you can delegate to him progressively harder jobs which will in themselves be a form of training. To protect yourself and him against his own inexperience let him make his earlier decisions on matters which would not disrupt the whole works if they went wrong.

Encourage people to think through their own problems. You can do this by turning people's questions back to them and asking them for their ideas on how a given problem should be solved.

Don't delegate to separate people jobs which overlap unless this is specifically recognized. Nobody likes to find that somebody else has been working on the job which he has been given. It seems to show a lack of trust.

Don't be a constant 'checker-upper'. Decide how you are going to appraise results, but remember how it feels to have someone constantly at your elbow watching you. Leave him to get on with the job.

Try to distribute your delegated work. Arrange for as many people as possible to take decisions. By giving everybody a chance you will spread the advantages and risks, and not overload one person.

Make the person's authority clear. If you give a person responsibility you must ensure that he has enough authority for carrying it through. So make sure that other people whose help he will need know that he has been given the job.

Consider when to delegate. When you are assigned a new employee, or when a system is changed, when a new job comes up—these are all good opportunities. But make a start now with your list of duties and begin offloading from today.

Delegate gradually. It may take a year to delegate all you can, so don't rush it.

Be patient. When you start delegating you will find that your workload is greater, because you have to train, guide and correct the employee to whom you are assigning the work. Once you have made the effort to do this, however, you begin to reap cumulative rewards.

Work towards a system of 'management by exception'. This means that your staff do not waste your time reporting about those things which are going normally, but only those things which are exceptions—whether good or bad. Provided the system is working properly you know that no news means everything is normal. There is no fail-safe on this, so you do have to check the really important issues periodically. The morning inspection is as good a time as any.

In order to find out if you are delegating enough, test yourself on the checklist in Fig. 12.2.

Fig. 12.2. Checklist on delegation

Questions	× √	Notes
1. Are you seldom interrupted by staff asking you about the job, what, why, how and who is to do it?		
2. Do you have to decide all matters or do your staff have some power of decision making?		
3. Do you seldom find yourself doing the job of one of your staff when he really ought to be doing it himself?		
4. Do you have time to plan your work and manage your staff properly?		
5. Are you good at organizing the job to be done and leaving the details to the man who is to do it?		
6. Do you avoid breathing down people's necks?		
7. Do you show confidence in your staff's ability?		
8. Do you avoid setting your standards so high that only you can attain them?		
9. Do you disclose details about the job, dispelling any unnecessary air of secrecy?		
10. How often do you allow your subordinates to do the thinking about a particular job as well as the doing?		
11. Do you always give enough information about the job so that, if things go wrong, the man responsible can use his own initiative to put them right?		
12. Do your subordinate supervisors have access to procedure guides, rulebooks, etc., so that they can take action on their own?		
13. Do you avoid habitually working longer hours than the people under you?		

Questions	× √	Notes
14. Are you seldom rushed off your feet?		
15. Do you delegate the right to be wrong?		
16. Do you ensure that there is full understanding between you and your subordinates about the requirements of the job?		
17. When you are away does the work go on normally?		
18. Is there good liaison between your department and others on delegated work?		
19. Have all the jobs been analysed and is each one being done by the right calibre person?		
20. Are the capabilities of each of your staff being fully used?		
21. Are there sufficient signatories and are the signing and authorization procedures efficient?		
22. Are the standardized form letters/memos up to date and are they being properly used?		

Questions

1. 'I could do it myself quicker than if I stopped to explain.' What is the fallacy of this argument if used too often?

2. Outline a programme for effective delegation within a department.

13. *The organization you work in*

During the last ten years take-overs, amalgamations, and company growth have meant that many supervisors today work within large and complex organizations. The supervisor is often no longer solely in charge of his department. There are planners, programmers, inspectors, progress chasers and large numbers of other specialists all having a say in how well, how soon, in what way, and at what cost, the product must be made. Sometimes it looks as though all these people are just passengers on the back of those who make the product, but this is a false picture. To understand the function of all these specialists it is useful to identify three main kinds of activity in industry, namely:

▷ the deciding,
▷ the systematic planning,
▷ the doing.

In smaller companies top management does the deciding and lower management and the employees carry out the doing with as much planning as time permits. In larger organizations top management still does the deciding but the systematic planning is done by specialists so that lower management and the production staff can devote their full energies to production.

If supervisors are to work well, particularly in these new huge and complicated industrial concerns, it is important for them to understand something about the principles of organization. Every supervisor is a practitioner in management and should know the theory of it if he is to do his job properly. For this reason I should first like to outline the main features of a typical company and then talk about some of the problems which may arise in the course of its work.

The structure of the organization

The shareholders

If you buy shares in a company you become a member of it and are entitled to a share of the profits which it makes. Shareholders have an Annual General Meeting to receive the chairman's report on the year's activities and to express their views on this subject and about future policy.

The function of the shareholders is to criticize and review.

The board of directors

This is responsible for the conduct of the business and for broad policy decisions. The results of their discussions are usually put into effect through the medium of the chief executive or managing director. Sometimes, however, other directors are also given executive powers and are thus known as 'executive directors'. They have the authority to give instructions directly to the managers below them without going through the managing director. This is a less common arrangement, and usually, therefore, the board's function can be defined as one of policy making.

The managing director

He is, as mentioned above, normally the person responsible for putting into effect the policies decided by the board, and for the day-to-day running of the company. He must:

Forecast. With regard to the formulated policy, he has to identify future trends and predict requirements.

Plan. Think out broadly what is to be done, how, when, and where and who will do it.

Organize. Organize resources of men, money, machinery, materials and plant, to put the plan into action.

Command. This means more than simply telling people what to do. He also has to tell people *why*, and motivate them so that they act enthusiastically, as well as intelligently and in the most economical way.

Coordinate. See that there is no overlap of duties, that no jobs are left undone, and that the left hand knows what the right hand is doing.

Control. Check how the plan is going and take action to put things right when they go wrong.

The managing director's function is essentially that of liaison between the policy makers (the board) and those who execute the policy (the management).

The management and operatives

The managing director is able to achieve production because his overall responsibility is broken down into manageable parts given to managers, specialists, superintendents, supervisors, chargehands and operators. There is no standard pattern of organization throughout industry—nothing to parallel the army's system—because one productive unit does not usually have to face the same problem in the same way as another.

The organization should be flexible, changing with the times and the new problems to be tackled. Too often businesses fail to do so due to shortsightedness or lack of courage in dealing with executives who have become firmly entrenched and resist change—restrictive practices are not only resorted to on the shop floor! To turn a blind eye to them at any level will only aggravate an already unsatisfactory situation.

Here are some typical organizational arrangements:

Line organization. Under this arrangement, shown in Fig. 13.1, orders all flow through the 'line' and each man can clearly see that he is reponsible to only one superior.

The organization should change with the times

Fig. 13.1

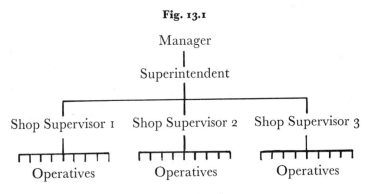

Functional supervision. Towards the end of the last century managers were, in some industries, already beginning to realize that the job was becoming too complex for a foreman to deal with all the technical, specialists' problems which come up in a day's work. F. W. Taylor, an American machine shop manager, introduced a new system of control at the Midvale Steel Company of Philadelphia in 1882–3. The object was to divide the foreman's job into its different functions and have a supervisor for each. From the men's point of view, they had five supervisors, four responsible for planning and one 'gang boss'.

Taylor developed the idea into a plan like the one in Fig. 13.2:

Fig. 13.2

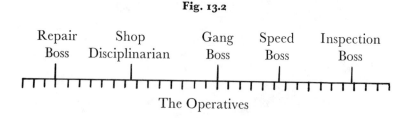

| Repair Boss | Shop Disciplinarian | Gang Boss | Speed Boss | Inspection Boss |

The Operatives

There were, in addition to these supervisors, clerks responsible for the administrative work that has to go with production. Although Taylor says it worked well, the system has not survived to the present day in the same form. Many managers feel that if you have too many supervisors, each allowed to give instructions to the same group of men, and each holding them responsible, misunderstandings develop and tensions between the various executives, with their different priorities, will split workshop loyalties.

The 'line and staff' organization. Under this plan you have only one supervisor in charge of a particular group of men. He is supported and advised by specialists. These are called staff officers. They do not carry any authority, and cannot give orders to the men, but must work only through the medium of the supervisor. He weighs up the specialists' advice and decides whether to accept or reject it in view of how he sees the complete picture.

The three themes outlined above suggest how authority and responsibility can be divided in an organization. The most common system nowadays is a mixture of all three.

It is generally accepted that a man cannot have more than one immediate superior and that, if specialists are needed, they should work through him rather than give orders directly to the employees. However, sometimes the specialist's advice is so crucial to the success of a particular operation, so unquestionable, that within strict limits he is in fact given authority to tell the men what to do without first telling their boss. Of course, it is vital that the supervisor should be very clear as to the extent of this authority, that this extent should be limited to a minimum, and that the specialist should never overstep it. If these precautions are taken, and provided you don't have too many functional specialists, it seems to work well. One good example of how it operates is when a ship's pilot takes over from the captain for a limited period and for the specific purpose of navigating a particular stretch of seaway or berthing the vessel.

Authority and responsibility

A football team would never go into action without being quite sure that the half-backs knew whom they were supposed to mark, and what the goalkeeper and forward line were meant to be doing, but plenty of firms neglect to take similar precautions.

Many companies have improved the effectiveness of their executives and advisory staff by producing position descriptions. When people's jobs are clearly defined they are not afraid to take a step in case they tread on someone's toes, because everybody knows where they stand and what they are supposed to do.

Many position descriptions today are based on the Management by Objectives (MbO) approach. Previously they took the form of a list of 20 or 30 duties and often did not distinguish between the vitally important responsibilities and the secondary ones. Now they are often called *position guides*, and specify broadly the five or six main functions or *key results areas* in which the manager has to perform well. They then establish the yardstick by which performance in each area shall be judged and the targets or objectives to be achieved over a given period. MbO position guides are dynamic and express action towards goals whereas the older type position description is static—more like an inventory of responsibilities.

Common weaknesses in companies' organization structures

Some companies are organizationally less efficient than they could be. Think of your own while you are reading this section. Identifying structural problems will help you to see the causes of some of your difficulties and where to watch your step.

Is the number of levels of authority kept to a minimum?

Fig. 13.3

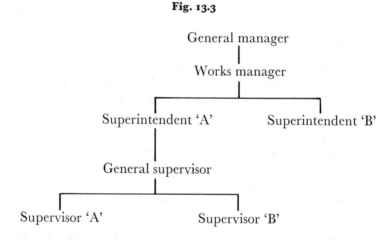

If there are too many links in the chain of authority from the general manager to the shopfloor (as shown in Fig. 13.3), the manager loses contact. More time is spent relaying messages, it takes longer to give decisions, and there seems to be less freedom of action because everything is decided somewhere up the line.

Whenever changes have to be made in work specifications or priorities, a long chain of command tends to make it harder to communicate. Staff soon feel despondent because they are so far removed from the top that they and their work don't seem to be in the limelight, except for criticism. There is also the extra cost to the company of employing more administrators than are really necessary.

Have managers or supervisors too many people to supervise?

Fig. 13.4

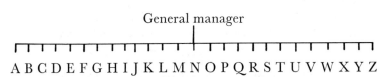

General manager

A B C D E F G H I J K L M N O P Q R S T U V W X Y Z

A number of widely different or unrelated jobs coming under the control of one man will make greater demands on his brains and experience than an equal number of similar ones would. But there is also clearly a limit to even the number of similar jobs one can supervise directly. Although there is no fixed number of people one man can supervise there are some useful points which tell you when there are too many. Watch for these signs: poor communication; employees' suggestions and ideas being overlooked; employees feeling that the supervisor does not count for much with the next man up; the tendency for rifts to develop between the supervisor and his manager. The cause of these could be that somebody has too wide a span of control.

Are managers tied to a particular process or technical expertise?

There are a number of ways of dividing up responsibility among managers. Too often a department will specialize in one particular process. Each has its pet technical job and you cannot introduce anything new unless you set up another department.

It is like a social club having a committee for darts, one for snooker, one for football and one for outings. Why not have a committee for indoor activities and one for outdoor activities, then you could introduce new pastimes? The same principle applies in industry. Perhaps processes could be grouped together under one head, who need not be an expert in each technology within his group, but knows enough about all of them, and enough about delegating, to guide and encourage his own subordinate experts. This was done in a printing company— one manager for preparing the printing surface with all its variations of letterpress, litho, etc., and one responsible for putting the print on the paper, whatever press was used. Now when a new process comes along, it will not be so difficult to introduce. The managers are already there to handle it and all they need do is to recruit their craftsmen and delegate.

Does the division of work bring similar jobs together or separate them?

When similar functions are grouped together, spans of control can be wider, and time, manpower, machinery and materials can be saved. Has each department, for example, developed its own paint shop with a range of paints, stencils, brushes, cleaning materials and its own labour? Perhaps there could be one large paint shop.

How does the organization's structure affect the work?

In some organizations authority is blurred, and two departments, sections, or operatives feel jointly responsible. In such cases the jobs could be looked at again under the headings shown in Fig. 13.5.

Fig. 13.5

Jobs now done	Problems arising	Organizational changes which might ease them

Does the organization provide for every major duty to be carried out?

Some organizations do not. An important duty takes second place in many an executive's crowded day. What duties have been partly overlooked in your company? Quality control? Staff development? Public relations? What organizational changes could be made in order to provide for their being properly carried out? Although you personally may not be in a position to change the structure, you can recognize the need for this, put forward suggestions when asked, and make allowances when you identify the root cause of problems which affect your job.

Are there watertight compartments and over-specialization?

Is your firm a company or a collection of departments which take an 'I'm all right Jack' attitude to everybody else? This sort of thing is bad for the firm as a whole, for the best interests of the company are not always served by acting in the best interests of one particular department. Try to see your section as a part of the whole.

The view from the shopfloor

It is usual to think of Jones, Smith, Brown and all the other names on the organization chart as being people who are helping the managing director. But you could think of it the other way round, starting with the people on the shopfloor who are actually making the product. For example, what support and help does the employee need in order to enable him to do his job better? What does everybody else do to help him? Is each one doing a full-time job which really puts power into the firm to make and sell its products, or has Parkinson's Law taken over? If you can think analytically about your organization (tempering your judgements with tact) the suggestions you put forward, and contributions you make as a member of the management team, will be wiser and sounder.

Does the organization put anybody in the position of taking orders from two bosses?

A man often has to serve more than one master in many modern organizations. Sometimes, for example, a clerk will have to work for two executives, because it is not possible to have two clerks on the payroll. But there will be problems. The ideal is one man, one boss. If the inefficiencies of dual subordination outweigh the advantages and economy, it seems to me there is a case for at least asking that each boss's authority should be made clear, and what happens in the event of a disagreement between them.

Conclusion

We are living in the age of the Organization Man. But this does not mean we all have to be unreasoning cogs in the machine. By understanding the mechanics of organizations you can play your part in keeping yours efficient.

Questions

1. In reviewing the duties of a personnel department it might be claimed that the supervisor's authority is undermined. Comment on this statement.

2. Name five defects in the structure of an organization, which could seriously affect the efficiency of supervisors, and explain why.

3. A supervisor should not have too many people to manage. What is likely to happen if he has, and what factors will influence the number he can control?

4. Should the supervisor consider himself as part of management? Please give your reasons.

14. *What you can do to improve work methods*

How efficient are the work methods in your department? You may have a work study department who have as one of their main duties the task of looking at the way in which jobs are done throughout the company and trying to rearrange the tools, workplace, sequence of operations and methods of operating so that less effort will be wasted and more effective work done. But don't leave it all to them.

Unless every supervisor and manager is aware of the basic principles involved in method improvement, the staff may find themselves wasting their energies on useless or inefficient tasks.

Here is an example of one such useless routine which came to light only through an industrial accident. The story began years ago when an operator was instructed to work a valve to blow steam down a pipeline into a catchpot outside. But 27 years ago, alternative arrangements were made and there was no longer any need to operate the valve. No one ever told the man to stop and he went on operating the valve until one day he opened it when somebody was walking by the catchpot outside. The pot was full of scalding steam and water splashed onto him. Only when the accident was investigated were the 27 years of useless work discovered.

It's no use waiting until work study identifies waste. In factories, offices and shops all over the country unproductive jobs are being carried out. Girls are filing away copies of documents that will never be referred to, clerks are keeping statistics that were needed five years ago when someone else was chairman but are not wanted by his successor, men are doing jobs machines could do, and many are doing them unsystematically. It all adds up to an appalling waste of resources and gives staff the impression that nobody cares very much what they do with their time.

How do you analyse jobs of work to find easier ways of doing them? If, as the work study people say, 'There's always a better way', how do you set about finding it?

Here is the procedure suggested by the originators of the 'Training Within Industry' scheme, now administered by the Department of Employment

This procedure for improving work methods is designed to make better use of manpower, machinery and materials. It doesn't depend on just casually spotting an inefficient part of the process, but on systematically breaking the procedure into steps, and challenging whether each step needs to be taken. If it is necessary, it challenges whether the action in question is being performed in the most effective way.

Could the whole job be eliminated?

It is important to ask this question first. The man who for 27 years worked the steam valve might have tried to find some more ingenious methods of doing it (a lever instead of a tap, a rope attached to the lever, etc.) but he would have been wasting his time if he had done so, because the job itself was unnecessary.

The six steps of method improvement

1. Choose the job.

Take any process carried out in your section which looks as though it could be done more safely, more easily, with less movement, or in such a way that it would eliminate bottlenecks.

2. Record the sequence of actions involved.

You have to note on paper an accurate breakdown of the steps or stages of the process. Tell the employee what you are trying to do. Consult him about the job and enlist his support in finding a better way of doing it. He will certainly accept a new method more readily if he has played a part in devising it.

3. Examine the method.

Fig. 14.1 shows the questions to ask.

4. Develop the new method.

Review all the ideas which your questions have raised. Eliminate as many unnecessary steps as you can, simplify those you cannot eliminate, and make sure the sequence is logical. Ensure that it is safe. Make a chart showing the new method and submit it for your boss's approval if you are satisfied that it is really a significant improvement.

5. Install the new method.

When you have received approval for it gauge the right time to put it in, e.g., before or after the holidays, New Year, when a particular person retires, perhaps even tomorrow. Convince all concerned and brief them or train them properly on the new procedure.

6. Maintain it.

Check up frequently at first. Is it achieving the expected result? If not, why not?—and what must be done to see that it does?

Many supervisors are good at doing their jobs as they are at present but not so many are actively trying to introduce changes for the sake of productivity, safety, or the elimination of bottlenecks. You may find at first that your idea is accepted with only lukewarm enthusiasm, but you must try to sell it if it is a good one, and not be too easily put off. If your boss is hesitant it is because he is asking himself whether he should stake his reputation on this new idea of yours. It is up to you to persuade him that he can!

Fig. 14.1. Job methods—the questioning technique

		Consider
What is achieved ?	Is it necessary ? Why ?	What other achievement would be better ?	Safety
Where is it done ?	Why there ?	What other place would be better ?	Design
When is it done ?	Why then ?	What other time would be better ?	Layout
Who does it ?	Why that person ?	What other person would be better ?	Equipment
How is it done ?	Why in that way ?	What other way would be better ?	Materials
		NOTE ALL IDEAS	

Other method study tools

Besides the 'questioning technique', as this is called, there are a number of other very useful tools for improving efficiency. These include process charts which give you a simplified picture of the job, bar charts showing labour utilization, string diagrams for measuring distances travelled in the course of the work, and many other ingenious ways of looking at the job and the effort involved. If you have never attended a work study appreciation course of about a week's duration, I would strongly recommend this to you.

Question

1. What is meant by the *questioning technique* in methods planning? What questions are asked?

15. *Cost reduction*

Not all the advice on cost reduction applies to every supervisor, so this chapter is divided into three parts:

Cost reduction for all supervisors. Everything in this section is likely to apply to you whatever kind of work you do.

Supplement for factory production supervisors. Here are some extra ideas which you will find helpful if you work on production in a factory.

Some useful cost accounting terms. These will be of value if you have to work with budgets or are interested in knowing more about cost accounting.

Cost reduction for all supervisors

What is increased productivity?

If a factory produces 1000 units a day at a cost of £10 000 and an extension is built so that it can produce 2000 units for £20 000 its production will double but its productivity will be the same. Productivity is the ratio of input to output and you raise it by getting proportionally more out than you put in. You can only do this by cutting the unit cost of production.

Why cost reduction matters

Any firm which cannot improve its productivity each year is really sliding backwards. Your company's product is competing with others making the same thing who are trying to take a greater share of the market. It is also competing with firms making different goods because the customer has only a limited number of pounds and an unlimited number of wants to satisfy. He will use his money on the things that give best value first, so if you make refrigerators you may be competing with anybody, from the carpet manufacturer to the television company. It won't do to cut prices by paring down dividend payments to shareholders either. In the first place, there isn't much payable after tax has been deducted and a sizeable sum has been ploughed back into the business, and dividend reduction may discourage people from investing in the firm next time it needs money to expand. If an investor cannot earn more than the interest on corporation loans, he is unlikely to put his money into industry, where the risk is greater.

The role of the cost accountant

The cost accountant produces facts and figures so that management can make the best use of the materials, men and machines available. He compares a new method of manufacture with the present one and tells you if it will save money. He produces figures showing how actual expenditure and performance compares with forecasted budgets or standard costs. The figures he produces are like the rev. counter, thermometer and speedometer, which tell the driver of an engine how it is running. The supervisor is the key man here. It is he, and not the accountant, who can save money.

If there are no proper control figures, a company can go seriously off the rails before anyone realizes that anything is wrong. If you are lucky enough to have access to cost data, make sure that you know how to interpret them. Ask the accountant to explain where your costs are high or out of line. Go through your budgetary returns with him and learn how to read your score. *Management is measurement*, and if somebody has given you the measurements it is up to you to learn how to interpret them. Incidentally, the information you receive from the system is only as accurate as the information you feed in, so be sure that you charge expenses to the correct account number.

How does the supervisor influence costs?

You can directly affect:

▷ how diligently people work;
▷ their skill;
▷ the methods they use;
▷ the time which is lost;
▷ the extra work which is sometimes done;
▷ the materials which are wasted.

Chapters 1, 2, 5 and 14 give guidance on the first three points listed above.

Cutting lost time

Your company's task is to deliver quality products at the time they are wanted and at the right price. If the job comes out in good time, you save on payroll and machine time, and so help in the long term to cut prices. Moreover, you help to keep the customer happy and he will want to buy more if the sales department can promise earlier deliveries. Time is often thrown away, but you do not notice this form of waste so much because it doesn't litter the floor. Yet accumulated lost minutes can cost thousands.

Wasted time and delay in your department may produce unnecessary expense in others. Here is how an assembly department in a factory could suffer, if previous departments were running late:

▷ idle time waiting for parts to arrive;
▷ overtime to make up for lost time to meet delivery dates;
▷ penalty payments to customers for late deliveries;
▷ air-freight charges on shortages which could not be shipped with machines.

Six ways to improve productivity

1. *Half jobs.* Sometimes a new responsibility comes along which doesn't really occupy a person for a whole day and yet somebody is assigned to it full time. It is important to have a look

at these half jobs now and again and see if two of them can be combined into one. Perhaps somebody doing a £4000 a year job spends a part of his time on work which a £2000 a year man could do. This may not be as wasteful as it looks if by so doing you avoid taking a new person on the payroll with all his overheads.

2. *Make sure the next job is ready.* Unless the next job is lined up, staff tend to slacken off their pace and effort to match the work in hand. Make sure that the next job is there and that they know it. ·

3. *Reducing material costs.* Encourage your staff to take care with small items as well as the expensive ones. Nuts, bolts, pencils, and paper-clips cost very little singly, but multiply them by a few hundred for the number of people wasting them and another few score for the number of times per year and it soon mounts up. Tell them about this sort of wastage. If you have to throw away useless materials or tools, let purchasing department know about it, because they may think that they have been getting a bargain. Moreover, they may be able to obtain credit from the suppliers. Perhaps you can also persuade your purchasing department to try for a different material, a casting instead of a machined piece, strips instead of sheets, or smaller sizes. Remember that when the job was set up the present material might have been the best or the only one they could find. Times have changed and now you can probably do better. Sometimes the product may be made at a great cost to the factory when it could be bought cheaper outside. Try to get costs and figures to support your argument if you think so.

You will have noticed how in supermarkets great piles of tins or carelessly heaped bars of soap are used to make the customer feel extravagant. Masses of materials have that psychological effect in the factory too, so counteract it by restoring your men's cost awareness. Persuade them to try to cut one more piece out of a length, or a sheet or a pound. Don't let them waste the first dozen yards on the start-up, or

let the first two gallons of fluid run off before they take what
they need.

4. *Fatigue costs money.* If you have a work study man, ask his
advice on how some of the jobs in your department could be
made less tiring. Many jobs are harder than they need be

Are tools and materials easy to reach?

because tools and materials are difficult to reach; a chair or bench of the wrong height can cause strain on the back and neck; trays of completed batches may be too big, too small, too heavy or too awkward; excessive time and effort may be used in hunting for tools or gauges. The work study man is trained to use a great many methods-study techniques for making jobs easier and faster.

5. *A question of teamwork.* Cutting costs is like most of management, a question of teamwork. Besides your cost accountant, remember that, among others, you can ask for the help of all these service departments:

▷ engineering,
▷ stores,
▷ purchasing,
▷ methods planning,
▷ industrial relations,
▷ quality control,
▷ production control, etc.

Above all, don't overlook the people nearest to the cost leaks—your own men on the shopfloor. One foreman I knew was wondering why Frank Gardner, an assembly worker, was twice as quick as the rest. Then he discovered that Frank had installed hooks on the upright at the back of his bench; all his tools were set out in the order he needed them, and he would reach for the one he wanted without looking up from his work. A suggestion scheme can bring out such ideas as these, create cooperation, and provide the men with a reward for their help.

By consulting the staff, you will spot wastage that could have been overlooked, you will make them cost conscious, and, above all, you will help to create a sense of partnership on the job.

6. *Learn how to do value analysis.* Value analysis, which is an extension of the methods-planning techniques mentioned

in chapter 14, means studying a product to see whether it can be made cheaper and still give the required service and performance. Many companies have made great savings with this approach. For example 77 per cent was cut off the cost of manufacturing a small spring in one firm and in another the cost of pump bases was reduced from £2·50 to 87½p.

A team consisting of departments such as design, production, purchasing and sales select a best-seller from the range of products or components and then go through the following stages:

(a) *Information stage*. Get all the data and information relevant to the product.

(b) *Speculation stage*.
Can job be done another way and at lower cost?
Can something else be used instead?
Can dimensions be reduced?
Can waste in manufacture be reduced?
Are correct limits or finishes specified?
Can standard components be used instead of specials?
Can we buy out cheaper? Can we make cheaper?
Can cheaper components be substituted to do jobs?
Can alternative material be used?
Let ideas pour out ('brainstorming').

This stage is carried out as a team discussion to which suppliers may also be invited so that they can make suggestions from their knowledge of their own products. It is important that no-one should hold an inquest as to why certain mistakes have not been spotted before, otherwise everyone will become too defensive to cooperate. While the ideas are being offered and listed, all present have to guard against their negative reactions such as 'They won't accept it', 'We've tried it', 'Why try it?', and 'What is wrong with our present way?'

(c) *Investigation stage*. The team breaks up and mulls over these ideas for a week or two.

(*d*) *Recommendation stage.* A meeting is held to assess ideas and decide which ones to put to management.

(*e*) *Implementation stage.* Before implementing the ideas which have been adopted, top management consults the unions in order to pave the way for acceptance on the shopfloor.

Value analysis is useful because nobody tends to look at products which have been going well for some time. Although the technique is really just organized commonsense, the discipline and teamwork of this approach lead to discoveries which individual intelligence would be unlikely to spot. Even if your company does not adopt value analysis in a formal way you can make use of the basic ideas behind it.

Supplement for factory production supervisors

If you are a production supervisor in a factory, try some of these additional tips

Machine-paced jobs with slack

Sometimes an operator is only working at half speed because the job is machine paced and it is running slowly. It is important to check up on machine speeds and see whether they are adjusted to give the best output without overworking the operator. Here an efficient rate-fixing department can help by fixing realistic piecework prices based on the right speeds.

Machine down time

There will be less down time if you develop in an employee a sense that this is his machine and encourage him to take a pride in it, do minor adjustments and keep it running. Let him know how much it cost to buy new. A man who takes pride in his £2000 car will probably value his £20 000 machine. You can train people to report suspicious machine noises or smells and so avoid serious damage. If the machine breaks down, tell the operator to:

An employee will take pride in 'his machine'

1. Give as much information as possible to the maintenance mechanic so that he can come prepared.

2. Show or describe to the mechanic the last piece off the machine.

3. Explain the symptoms.

4. Say whether it has happened before.

If he himself caused the accident he should be encouraged to admit how he did it, because in this way he can save wasted time in faultfinding. If a machine frequently goes out of action, talk to your maintenance department about why it is costing you so much. It may pay to keep a record of how much time it is out of action. Preventive maintenance could also be the answer. Perhaps it would even pay to have a new machine. The maintenance man doesn't always know how much it is costing you, and you may have to show him some figures to prove your case.

Make sure that staff report waiting time

Some departments have workcards which show waiting time. If yours has, are you sure that your men record all their down time and don't hide it because they think it may cause you trouble? It helps if waiting time can be recorded in categories like this:

▷ wait for work;
▷ wait for materials;
▷ wait for supervisor;
▷ wait for inspector;
▷ wait for fork lift truck, etc.

Many supervisors spend 15 minutes a day looking through the workcards of the men in their department. By doing this you can find out about any delays or hold-ups before these returns leave the department and arrive on the desk of somebody else who might ask awkward questions.

If a piecework system is operating in your department, insist that claims for waiting time are put in immediately. If you get an omnibus claim at the end of the week, you cannot remember all the details and in any case it is too late for any remedies.

Cut down on unnecessary work

One form of extra work results from wasted set-up time when a rush job comes along and just has to go through on a particular machine which is all set for production, or which is going flat out, but you have to break the run. There is not much you can do about this except perhaps to persuade your boss to allow you to make up, in slack time, some of the most often used spares.

Sometimes you can persuade production control to allow you to combine production orders which are similar. Perhaps the greatest hidden cost is in what happens to the staff's attitude to the work . . . 'Why bother to break our necks on this job . . . we shall have to undo all our work again.' 'Why should we bother to try and save a few pennies in time? . . . those people up in the office are throwing away hundreds of pounds.' 'The company is a shambles, the left hand doesn't know what the right hand is doing.'

You can and must combat this feeling. You will have delivery and priority problems every day that your firm has customers. You must recognize these are the circumstances you have to work under, and help the team to adopt the right attitude towards them. Try to streamline methods of changeover. Rearrange your set-up sequences. Sometimes the answer is in training a more versatile crew. Many firms make a point of recording set-up time so that the cost of excessive changes can be accurately measured against the benefits.

Rework

Scrap means wasted material and time spent doing the job again. Check whether the trouble is with the tools. Are implements blunt or inaccurate? Measuring or recording instruments in need of adjustment? Get the toolroom to routine-check tools before issue. Find out from the toolroom who is misusing them, and without making anyone feel that you are getting at him, give some tips on tool care. If you have repeated defects of a similar kind, track down the cause. Get back to the person who is producing scrap and set him on the right lines. Encourage operators not to hide known rejects among a trayful of good parts. Train them to detect a trend towards spoilage (e.g., punch holes deteriorating with each press-movement) and take action *before* the first reject is produced, rather than after. Scrap should be declared at once, otherwise further operations may be wasted later and time lost if replacements have to be ordered.

Standards of finish

The security officer wanted a piece of wood to stick under the back of the key cabinet to stop it from rocking on the uneven floorboards. He asked the carpenter's shop for a block $\frac{1}{2}'' \times 2'' \times 6''$. In came a piece of oak four days later, sanded and varnished, neat enough to serve as the works director's paperweight. It sounds fantastic, but how often do you fail to specify standards, and as a result receive something which is too good or too bad?

Have you ever known one department to put a superb finish on a part which is going to be painted over in assembly? If the specifications say 'fine', how fine is that? You may need to ask for some proper standards—perhaps even a set of samples if you often have doubt about the type of finish needed.

Poor liaison with the engineering department

Production men sometimes curse 'those impractical pencil-mechanics in the engineering drawing office,' but don't let this go as far as letting them produce something which is obviously not going to be right. Persuade somebody from the office to come down to see the headache which their blueprint is causing. In one engineering works they often made changes to specifications on the floor without telling the engineering department. Engineering naturally carried on in ignorance making the same type of error in their drawings. Don't rely on a word-of-mouth agreement with them to do the thing differently. Try to have the drawings changed if they are wrong. Ask the engineers to put in all necessary dimensions; the man on the shopfloor should not have to work out geometry problems. While we are on the subject of drawings, make sure that obsolete ones are not left in the men's lockers as often scrap is caused by not working to the latest drawing.

Some useful cost accounting terms

Companies vary in their attention to budgetary control and standard costing. Some supervisors never see a budget at all, and in fact sometimes the company itself has only the most simple kind of costing system. On the other hand, your firm may feel it is important to provide cost information to all managers and supervisors and encourage front-line supervision to interpret and act on it.

If you don't understand fully what these figures and returns mean or how you can use them, ask the cost accountant or your department head to go over it with you.

The following are some useful accounting terms. Read them up and then check your understanding of them by answering the quiz at the end of the chapter.

Labour costs

The direct labour cost is the gross wages paid to the staff who work directly on the product, e.g , grinder, lathe operator, extrusion press operator, etc.

The indirect labour cost. The timekeeper, supervisor and floor-sweeper are necessary to production but their work is contributory rather than direct. Their wages and salaries are indirect labour costs.

Material costs

The direct material cost is the value of the materials which go into the product. They include, for example, the plastic, steel and rubber in your car.

The indirect material costs are the costs of such things as grinding wheels and lubricants. You could not do without them, but they never form part of the finished article.

Sometimes there are borderline cases which might be classed as direct or indirect, whether under the heading of labour or material. Your cost accountant will give a ruling if asked.

Overhead costs

These are all the indirect labour and indirect material costs from your department and others, plus managers' salaries, the cost accountant and all the service departments. Rent and rates come into this category and so do all your firm's expenses which cannot be classified as direct materials or labour.

Variable indirect overheads

These are items which vary sharply in proportion to the amount of throughput and include oil and lubricants, cutting tools and machine fuel; and on the labour side, the wages of truck and crane drivers, labourers and sweepers.

Fixed indirect overheads

These do not vary much whatever the throughput and include, on the materials side, for example, replacement lamps for factory lighting; and on the wages side, such items as the wages of the night watchman or telephone switchboard girl. Rent, rates and depreciation are also classed as fixed overheads.

Budgetary control

Budgetary control is a system of forecasting an itemized summary of the expenditure of an organization or department over a period. This is followed by regular reports showing the rate of spending.

Standard costing

This amounts to budgeting the cost per item or number of items under 'normal' conditions. Once standard costs are fixed, you can compare them with the money spent as the job progresses and if you find that you are overspending you can find out why and then decide what to do about it. Standard costing also enables the firm to predict accurately what the product will cost and so give the customer more competitive, but safer, estimates.

Break even (recovery of overheads)

If a television factory produces only one set a day, the cost of producing would include, besides the direct costs, the whole of that day's indirect labour and materials (overheads)— probably £30 000. The break-even point for recovery of overheads is reached when enough sets are produced to share the overheads and when direct costs are added, make neither a loss nor a profit.

Figure 15.1 shows an example of a television factory where the variable cost may be £300 per set (direct wages, direct materials and variable overheads) and the fixed expenses £20 000 per day with a selling price (ex factory) of £500.

The break-even point is 100 sets per day since, at that output, the sales value equals the total cost. If the output falls to 90 sets

Fig. 15.1. Checklist on cost consciousness

Output per day (sets)	90	100	110	120
	£	£	£	£
Variable cost £300 each	27 000	30 000	33 000	36 000
Fixed cost	20 000	20 000	20 000	20 000
Total cost	47 000	50 000	53 000	56 000
Selling price @ £500 each	45 000	50 000	55 000	60 000
Loss per day	2000	—	—	—
Profit	—	—	2000	4000

per day, there is a loss due to unrecovered fixed overheads. If it rises above 100 a day a profit is made and it increases steadily from then onwards.

Those are the costing terms you are most likely to come across. Now try the quiz. Check your answers and if you get some wrong go back over the notes and see why.

Quiz on cost terms

1. How would you classify the cost of cloth in a tailoring factory?
2. How would you classify the wages of a fork-lift truck driver in your department?
3. 'The break-even point (recovery of overheads) is reached when the overheads divided by the units produced = the selling price.' Is this true or false?
4. Would you classify as a direct or indirect labour cost the wage of a maintenance electrician?
5. What is the term used for overhead costs:
   (a) Which rise with the number of units produced?
   (b) Which remain fairly static however many are produced?
6. Standard costing predicts the cost of each item or batch. Is this statement true or false?

Answers are on the next page.

Answers to quiz

1. Direct material cost.
2. Indirect labour cost.
3. False. What about the direct material and direct wages?
4. Indirect labour.
5. (a) Variable overheads.
   (b) Fixed overheads.
6. True, provided that the variances from budgeted standard cost are taken into account, e.g., wage awards, etc.

Questions	$\times \sqrt{}$	*Notes*
1. Do the staff work diligently?		
2. Do you ensure good timekeeping and are you yourself a good timekeeper?		
3. Do you make sure that there is full usage of equipment and staff?		
4. Do you keep overtime to the minimum necessary?		
5. Do you have the right number of people, not too few, nor too many?		
6. Do you try to ensure that there are no 'half-jobs'?		
7. Do you seek to change any methods which are unduly time wasting?		
8. Do you seek to change methods which are unduly tiring?		
9. Are the staff properly trained?		
10. Do they show cost consciousness?		
11. Do you ensure that they are not left short of materials, equipment, etc.?		
12. Is little time wasted through equipment being out of action?		

Questions	×✓	Notes
13. Do your staff always report delays and interruptions to the work flow?		
14. Do you check on it to try to remove the causes?		
15. Are you as careful about company STD costs as you would be on your telephone at home?		
16. Do you know the cost of the equipment and materials which your department uses?		
17. Is serious pilfering eliminated?		
18. Does bad equipment seldom cause scrap?		
19. Do you track down and put right recurrent causes of scrap?		
20. Do you avoid putting too much effort into achieving perfection on jobs which do not demand it?		
21. Are standards high enough where they should be?		
22. Do you always try to cut wasted work by achieving better liaison with other departments?		
23. Do people guard against small but frequent wastage in your department?		
24. Are you careful to see that lights, heaters, machinery etc., are not left on unnecessarily?		
25. Do you try to save the company money by talking to the purchasing officer about quality standards, or materials?		
26. Do you guard against extravagance resulting from 'seeing plenty around'?		
27. Do you plan staff holidays in order to arrange the minimum use of expensive temporary staff from agencies?		

Questions	X √	Notes
28. Do you actively obtain help from other departments in reducing costs? ▷ the departments for which you provide a service ▷ accounts ▷ stores ▷ purchasing ▷ organization and methods/work study ▷ personnel, etc.		
29. Do you ask your staff for their ideas on cutting costs? 30. Have you a working knowledge of the main principles of work study/methods planning?		

Questions

1. What is standard costing?

2. What are the aims of a cost system in a factory? What information about costs is of value to the supervisor?

3. Explain what is meant by budgetary control and show the part which a supervisor can be expected to play in the operation of such a system.

4. Outline the ways in which waste can arise in the use of materials and show the main ways in which this waste could be reduced to a minimum.

5. Describe the steps which could be taken to improve productivity in your department.

16. *Some special aspects of supervision*

Your deputy and you

It is very important to sort out with your deputy the duties you expect him to carry out, and what authority he is going to be given in order to do so. Agree with him the jobs that you want him to regard as his responsibility, those you will normally tackle, and those which need your joint attention.

Salary

Do you know how much he earns, and do you have any say in the raise he will have at the end of the year? You hope that the man you work for will influence the amount you are paid and what the firm thinks of you. Otherwise there would be less of an incentive for you to make sacrifices and put in an extra effort on the job. The same thing applies to your deputy.

His authority

Do you ever step in and correct him in front of the staff when he has given instructions? Do you back him up in the decisions he makes? Remember it isn't enough just to appoint him deputy; you must show that you respect his position if you expect the others to do so.

Put his name forward

His future

Will he ever become a supervisor? If he does a good job, do
you ensure that higher management hears about it? Would you
release him to another department if he could obtain quicker
promotion there? Would you put his name forward? What
training does he need to be able to do his present job better, and
what preparation will he need for the next job up? (See
chapter 5 on training.)

You can draw up your plans for him (see Fig. 16.1):

Fig. 16.1

Development Plan

Name ....

PRESENT TRAINING NEEDS	COMPLETION DATE
Operating G6 m/c.	1 March.
Setting T36.	31 March.
Interpreting drawings.	15 May.
Materials ordering procedure.	31 August.
Payroll administration, etc.	30 September.
TRAINING FOR PROMOTABILITY	COMPLETION DATE
Supervision course.	When available this year.
Budgetary system.	1 October.
Work study appreciation course, etc.	By end of year.

What special considerations are there in supervising women?

If you have been supervising women for any time at all you will know how important it is to be impartial, because they so easily suspect you of having favourites. Women tend to be emotional, so you will need to take it philosophically when you get a display of tears, and not assume that this is proof positive that you are the worst thing that has happened to womankind since Dr Crippen. In one sense when emotions are so clearly displayed, it does make the job easier: you know where you stand and can take the necessary action to put things right.

Motivation

People of either sex devote themselves most wholeheartedly to whatever interests them most. Too many supervisors are ready to say that the girls have no interest at all in the job, and yet they haven't bothered themselves to stimulate it. In my experience, women can display an infinite capacity for involvement in a task that is worth while. They want to be recognized, and they value their individuality even more than men do. Perhaps it is because historically a man's job has been to cooperate in a group to make a living or defend the community, while the woman's role has been to occupy a key role, uniquely, within the family.

The changing role of women in society

While women still occupy a unique position in the family, their role is changing to encompass more activities outside the home and partial responsibility for breadwinning. (Some women have full financial responsibility for young children or dependent elderly relatives.) During the last five years particularly there have been many more working mothers, and given a little consideration over the problems they may have through combining working with raising a family, they can represent a very conscientious, reliable influence in your team. This is because they are motivated by financial necessity or the need to have contacts outside the home.

So remember that, among your women employees, a number

will be going home each night to domestic tasks and responsibilities, maybe even anxieties. Find out if they have any special worries, like a sick child or an ailing elderly relative, and show your concern. You will be rewarded in terms of loyalty and application.

If your company operates flexible working hours it can recruit and suit more people who are in this position. Where there is no official company policy of timekeeping flexibility it can be worth employing part-timers. These are ideas you might put forward.

Another influence affecting all working women is the publicity being given to the Women's Lib. movement. While not actively supporting the movement by consigning their bras to the factory boiler, many women feel strongly about the need for changes regarding their rights. Be prepared for your women workers to be more militant in standing up for what they consider their rights, than, say, a few years ago. There may be wage differences between the sexes because of a difference in the nature of work performed, but do all you can to see that the women you supervise are not discriminated against over other benefits. Be prepared for an increase in the number of requests you receive for equal pay. The new law will put the pressure on.

The law and the employment of women in factories

(The figures given here apply to the five day week. There is a slight difference for six days.)

Hours. Women's working hours are limited by law so that they are not allowed:
1. To work more than 10 hours a day,
2. Or more than 48 hours a week,
3. Or more than $4\frac{1}{2}$ hours without a break.

Overtime. Their overtime hours are limited to:
1. Six hours a week.
2. 100 hours in 25 weeks.
(Total working hours in any one day must not be more than $10\frac{1}{2}$.)

Nightwork. They are not allowed to work between 10 p.m. and 5 a.m.

NB: Many of these conditions can be waived by agreement between the firm and the Department of Employment Factory Inspectorate, but do not contravene any of these stipulations unless you are sure that a special agreement of this kind has been made.

Other limitations. There are also a few other legal restrictions on the employment of women: for example, they are not allowed to work in a factory until four weeks after giving birth. You should check with your personnel officer if you have any doubts in your mind about points like these.

The older employee

Britain's population, like that of every other advanced and industrialized country, is getting older. In 1947 10·5 per cent of the population were aged 65 and over, but in 1980, 16 per cent of the population will come into that age group. This need not be a bad thing.

The long-established firm with a reputation has achieved it through the efforts of the oldsters. Although their work may have left plenty of room for improvement, every supervisor should have the humility to recognize that the innovations he wants to make may well have been impossible but for the pioneering that went before.

You CAN teach an old dog new tricks

Tests have shown that the memory is at its best between the ages of 15 and 30. But whereas it is easier to engrave new ideas in a young mind, the older a person becomes, the more experience and knowledge he has with which to associate the new material which he is being taught. It is as though there were in the mind more 'hooks' on which to hang the new ideas. The older worker also tends to be more responsible and conscientious, besides being less susceptible to distractions.

Other assets he has are:

Safety. Given work within his powers, he has fewer accidents.

Timekeeping. He has usually drilled himself effectively on this over the years.

Absenteeism. When he is away through sickness, he does tend to be off work longer, but his absences aren't so frequent.

Loyalty and steadiness. There aren't many old rolling stones.

Can a man over 55 do heavy work?

In a large scale survey carried out by the Industrial Society—
'The Employment of Elderly Workers'—it was found that in
certain heavy industries a high proportion of men in their fifties
and sixties were doing heavy work quite comfortably. It was a
question of having grown accustomed to it.

Certainly it is dangerous to generalize too much about the
veterans and many examples exist to prove that a man is as old
as he feels. But here is a guide to the kinds of work for which
staff in this age group are most often suited:

Fig. 16.2

Elderly employees are most suited to:	*They are least suited to:*
Work needing accuracy and sustained attention, but not speed.	Fast work under pressure.
	Work in competition with younger people.
Work which is done sitting and in good light.	
	Working in excessive heat or cold.
Work on which it is not necessary to learn new skills—except very simple ones.	Heavy work, unless used to this all their lives.
Working in a group of similar age but not necessarily cut off from younger people.	Work needing nimble fingers or good eyesight (unless they are used to it).

Preparing for retirement

Is retirement the end of a meaningful life? If you have older
employees in your department with this fear in their minds, ask

your personnel officer what help can be given. There may be a company policy which provides for retaining them in employment, or he may be able to refer you to such local sources of guidance as the Citizens' Advice Bureau or the local authority adult education classes where courses are sometimes presented for people approaching retirement.

Useful booklets on this subject are:

Enjoying Retirement, Dr Patricia Shaw, Industrial Society.
You and Your Pension, Betty Ream, Industrial Society.

Questions

1. How far is the supervisor responsible for the training and career progression of his deputy? What can he do to help him?

2. Explain three important points to bear in mind when supervising women staff.

3. What are the likely advantages and disadvantages of having in your section an employee who is nearing retirement?

17. *Planning and managing your time*

Planning substitutes thinking for worry

Planning everyday work

Make time for planning

When you are planning you are not actually producing but preparing to produce. It is tempting to say this is time-wasting, and dive straight in, thinking that it is better to press on rather than to sit and consider. Those who do this often get fair results just because they are boiling over with energy and they certainly look busier, but they are not always working as effectively as they might.

People who don't plan waste *manpower* because people are left idle; they waste *materials* because ordering is haphazard, and hasty work on materials which have arrived late leads to spoilage; they waste *machine time* because the equipment is not used to the full; and they waste *space* because incoming or outgoing work in progress piles up. Poor planning is also harmful to morale because nobody likes to do unnecessary work as a result of a time-wasting, ill-thought-out system.

Inadequate planning can even go so far as to cause nervous breakdowns, as Doctor John Stokes, Professor of the Graduate School of Medicine, University of Pennsylvania, pointed out. He said that when you have to deal with a neurotic you can very often find in his mind 'the sense of *must* or *obligation*; the unending stretch of things ahead that simply have to be done'. We can't do much to reduce the amount of work we have to get through, but we can master it by organizing it, establishing priorities, delegating and tackling things systematically. You may consider that with a full head of steam you can go through your workload without planning, but how promotable are you on that basis? Your superior may be looking for somebody whose attributes in his present job fit him for the next one up, so use *forethought* as well as sheer drive.

Work out simple systems for frequently recurring jobs

Instead of having to think out the sequence of events to be followed in the case of—say—a power failure, or a shutdown for preventive maintenance, work out the best system for dealing with a contingency and train your people to use it. In this way you will be able to delegate more. Perhaps there is a precedent and somebody has already done this job before, so check and see.

In the production department of one of the Shell oil fields in Venezuela, an ingenious system was devised to shorten the time it took to replace the drive belts which worked the well-head pumps. Operators used to have to go to the particular well whose drive belt had worn and snapped, measure the length (they were non-standard) required, return to base and have a belt of that size cut, then drive to the well again and fit the belt. This system was changed by the supervisor in charge who made a list of all the wells and a note of the belt size required or each. Now when there is a breakage the operator looks up the well number, checks the belt size, makes one up, and goes out to fit it, thus making only one journey instead of two.

Consider using a year-to-view organizer

These are wall charts, about three feet across by two feet high, divided into months and days showing the whole year. They are excellent for programming activities over long periods, showing public holidays and people's vacations, and giving you an overall view of your commitments so that you can see when your peak periods of activity occur, and when you will be free to undertake special assignments. They are also useful for

Fig. 17.1. Inspection schedule

Item	Date checked									Why is this item being followed up so much?	Why is this item being neglected?
	1/4	8/4	17/4	10/5	20/5	12/6	14/6	26/6	17/7		
Hand tools	1/4									←	
First-aid pack	2/4										←
Gangways	3/4	4/5	13/5	21/6							
Bench tops	3/4	6/5	10/6	19/6							
Air lines	2/4	7/5	13/6								
Belt drives	3/4	7/5	10/6	19/6							
Spares kit	3/4	14/4	28/5	21/5			Smith weak—see him. →				Pencilled note to be erased when action taken.	
Fire extin.	4/4	9/5	10/6	27/6							
Emer. exits	2/4	8/5	14/6	No follow-up needed for one month. →							
Prod. tickets	4/4	29/4	10/5	27/6						Spaces left for insertion of new items.	
Toilets	4/4	10/5	21/6								

Reproduced by kind permission of the Industrial Society Inc.

reviewing past activities if you are ever asked for that sort of information.

Use checklists

A salesman who has to make frequent trips away from home does not leave it to memory every time he packs his case. In the wardrobe there is a checklist of every item that must go in. Packing is a simple job—he just checks off socks, pants, shirts, toothbrush, etc., and makes sure that he doesn't forget a thing. This is also an aid to delegation—his wife can do it. Perhaps checklists could save you a lot of mental effort. They can be used for lists of tools and materials for special jobs, safety inspections and so on.

Checklists can remind you of those periodic jobs. Figure 17.1 shows an example of how one supervisor drew up an inspection schedule and earned himself the reputation of never missing a trick.

Draw up a schedule

Many supervisors keep a list of pending jobs on their desk. Some find it useful to note them on a piece of paper on a portable clip-board, hanging by their desk. Write down everything you have pending, then as you complete each item tick it off. When you do this you can adequately sort out priorities. There are always a number of duties which, in a matter of seconds, you can have under way and which will get completed automatically. Others you can delegate, others must follow in sequence behind something else on your list, and perhaps some can wait a few days. The point is that the order in which you tackle jobs is practically as important as how well you complete them, so a few minutes spent in arranging priorities is a good investment.

Try to make time for non-routine creative jobs, undertaken on your own initiative, but not, of course, without management's approval. Look at your different kinds of work along the lines shown in Fig. 17.2.

Fig. 17.2

Classification	List of jobs	Comments
Regular	1............... 2............... 3............... 4............... 5............... 6............... 7............... 8............... 9............... 10..............	See that these are done well.
Irregular (Periodic)	1............... 2............... 3............... 4...............	Handle promptly. Try to remove causes.
Special (Occasionally handed out by supervisors)	1............... 2............... 3...............	See to these and do them well.
Creative (New departures, projects, prototypes)	1............... 2............... 3............... 4............... 5...............	How well you do these is really crucial. Promotion often depends ultimately on this sort of work.

Keep a list of pending jobs

Are you a lark or an owl?

Tackle tough jobs when you are at your best, and this does not necessarily mean first thing in the morning. Everyone is a *lark* or an *owl* to a greater or lesser extent. If you accept whichever you are and schedule your day accordingly you will accomplish more.

Larks come in full of bounce and ready to face the day, able to tackle the hardest job with gusto. Owls at this time are still struggling to get their eyes open and have to fortify themselves with a cup of coffee before they can tackle the day's work at all.

If you are the latter, save your most demanding jobs for later in the day and use the early morning to get routine stuff out of

Are you a lark or an owl?

the way. Owls are still going strong later on when the larks are worn out.

Planning the big job

The schedule of pending items is a good method of deciding priorities when you have a large number of small jobs to do, but how do you go about planning a big project like organizing, say, the move of your department's equipment and machinery to a new location? The four steps outlined below should help you with major projects.

Define the objective

In the example given above it would be 'Move all the machinery from department A to department B and have it operational in 24 hours from Saturday at noon.'

Do a job breakdown

Divide your paper vertically down the middle with a line and write in the left-hand column all the things you can think of which you will have to consider about the move (see Fig. 17.3). Don't worry about the order, just write them down as they come into your mind, like this:

Fig. 17.3

Item	Detail
Positioning of machines	
Transport	
Manpower for move	
Power (disconnect and connect)	
Fitters	

When you have thought of as many items as you can, pick out the one which others depend on, and start your detailed planning of that. Then begin asking the questions: what, why, who, how, where, when? They are like a set of spanners, because you use them when they fit. In this case 'Positioning of machines' comes first. Question WHY? doesn't apply. Question WHO?—who can advise me about the new lay-out? Answer: check with engineering department. Questions WHAT? WHEN? HOW? WHERE? do not apply, so leave them out and go on to the next point.

Now the job-breakdown sheet looks like Fig. 17.4.

Fig. 17.4

Item	Detail
Positioning of machines	
Transport	
Manpower for move	
Power (disconnect and connect)	
Fitters	
1. Positioning of machines	Check with engineering dept.

The next point could be 'transport'. Question WHY? doesn't need asking. Question WHO?—who can help with transport? Answer: transportation department. WHAT?—what is needed? Answer: 1 Mack truck with winch, 1 fork lift. WHEN?—when do we want them? Answer: fork lift truck at Saturday noon shutdown. Mack truck at 2 p.m. (2 hours after shutdown to allow time for fitters to disconnect and unbolt No. 1 machine).

At this point you may remember the need for a lunch break so you put that on your list of items.

Back to using the 'spanners' on the transport question. There is one more to ask. WHERE?—where are the trucks to report? Answer: outside A machine shop. Now the chart looks like Fig. 17.5

Fig. 17.5

Item	Detail
Positioning of machines Transport Manpower for move Power (disconnect and connect) Fitters Lunch break	
1. Positioning of machines	Check with engineering department.
2. Transport	Consult transportation department. 1 fork lift truck noon Saturday 1 Mack truck 2 p.m. Saturday To report outside A machine shop.

Now the next question—'Manpower'.

Question WHY? doesn't need asking. WHO—who should supply labour?—maintenance department for fitters, electrical department for power arrangements, transportation department for labour gang (probably six men) and drivers. WHEN?—electrician to have a preliminary look today. Fitters needed on Saturday at noon, labour gang needed at 2 p.m. WHERE?—A shop. Questions HOW? and WHAT? don't need asking.

The planning sheet has gone to the stage shown in Fig. 17.6.

Fig. 17.6

Item	*Detail*
Labour	2 fitters—maintenance department; required 12 noon Sat.
	Electrician—electrical department; required Mon. 4 p.m. and 12 noon Sat.
	6 labourers—transportation department; required 2 p.m. Sat.
	All report to A shop.

. . . and so it goes on through all the remaining questions.

Inform and consult all concerned

Check with the heads of departments on whose services you will have to rely. This includes engineers, maintenance, electrical and personnel department (for overtime authorization). Tell them your plan and ask for their help and suggestions. See them personally. Where appropriate let them have notes in writing.

Follow up

After your plan has been carried out, ask yourself what, if anything, went wrong, and learn from your mistakes. Take prompt action to remedy whatever it was that did not go according to plan.

Ensure your timing is right

The army teaches its officers and NCOs to use the 'D-day minus' principle. When there is a sequence of events which must take place before the job itself begins, work back in time, fixing the deadline for each preparatory stage. Suppose your department has to produce a sample of its work for an exhibition at Olympia in London on Friday, 28 May. 28 May is D-day, so the assembly and erecting on site of your part of the exhibition must be completed by D-day minus two, in order to allow a safety margin.

All components must be transported a day before that which is D-day minus three.

Manufacture and inspection must be completed on D-day minus four. And so you carry on until finally you arrive at the date for starting. Don't forget to keep everybody informed—sometimes it is worth giving them a plan along these lines:

20 May—making of components completed.

23 ,, —assembly completed.

25 ,, —transport to London.

26 ,, —erecting on site completed.

27 ,, —Marketing Manager inspects stand at Olympia.

28 ,, —exhibition opens.

Critical Path technique

Critical Path (network analysis and P E R T are variants) is an aid to the planning, coordination and control of major jobs. You draw a diagram showing the critical path for the project, that is the sequence of operations which must wait upon each other. If you add up the time each takes you can estimate the earliest completion date.

For example, in decorating a room you have to paint the woodwork before you paper the walls. If the painting takes a day, drying takes a day, and papering takes two days, the total time for the project is four days. If the ceiling needs a coat of emulsion this job can be done at the same time as the woodwork so that it will not lengthen the critical path. But if the householder is fussy and wants the woodwork sanded before the paint is applied, he obviously cannot have this done at the same time as the painting or papering, so it will lengthen the critical path. (See Fig. 17.7)

Fig. 17.7

With a more complicated project things are less obvious than this, so the diagram is essential. It helps you to see your priorities more clearly, as any delay on the critical path must receive immediate attention. If there should be a delay on one of these jobs, the diagram helps you to spot the implications of it and accurately revise your completion date. Suppose the householder insisted on the sanding of the woodwork and yet still required the job to be ready in four days. You could save a day by using quick-drying paint at the following stage.

Develop the right habits

The morning inspection

Many supervisors find it a useful timesaver to go round their department once a day to keep in touch. Inspections will prevent you from overlooking things which you might forget. They will make you available for solving problems or answering questions, enable you to check on the progress of newcomers to your department and provide a fixed opportunity for people to see you so that they are not always interrupting at odd times during the day.

Cultivate the delegating habit

Think who could do the job for you. Chapter 12 gives advice on this.

Tell people who need to be informed

When you receive instructions or think up a plan, remember to ask yourself 'Who must I tell about this?'

Make notes

It is wise to make a regular habit of noting points for action. Always make these in the same spot to avoid hunting around for the particular back of an envelope where it was jotted down for convenience. Some people use a pad of tear-off slips with a carbon paper inserted so that they can give people written instructions and keep a note for reference.

Put things in the same place

Many supervisors who as craftsmen were meticulous about how they put their tools back in their kit box, do not carry their good habits into the office, where they are just as necessary.

Before leaving the subject of planning I should like to tell you of an incident which happened at the Industrial Society a few years back. Mrs Byers in the print room would always do a job for you 'yesterday' if you really wanted it, but the workload was impossible even for her on this particular day. 'Laura, I wonder if you could print me a hundred copies of these notes by tomorrow?' She said nothing but looked over her glasses at the door. The way out? No! There was a little note there. (We cannot find out who wrote it, but it is too good to leave out of this book so, with acknowledgements to the author, here it is.)

I belong to no age for men have always hurried.
I prod all human endeavour.
Men believe me necessary—but falsely.
I rushed today because I was not planned yesterday.
I demand excessive energy and concentration.
I over-ride obstacles, but at great expense.
I illustrate the old saying 'haste maketh waste'.
My path is strewn with the evils of overtime,
    mistakes and disappointments.
Accuracy and quality give place to speed.
Ruthlessly I rush on.
I am a rush job.

Fig. 17.8. Checklist on planning and organizing

Questions	×√	Notes
1. Do jobs come out to time and to the right standard?		
2. Does the work run smoothly?		
3. Are you able to predict fluctuations?		
4. Do you have plans for making the best use of your labour at off-peak times?		

Questions	× √	Notes

5. Is there evidence of your planning?
6. Do you distribute work in the most effective way?
7. Do you decide priorities correctly?
8. Do you delegate as far as possible?
9. Do you make the best use of service departments?
10. Do you get materials on hand before time?
11. Does your department cooperate effectively in the team as a whole?
12. Thinking back over any recent wastage of manpower, materials, machine time, or floor space in your department, are you *sure* it could not have been avoided?
13. Do you avoid wasting time looking for documents, tools, equipment, etc.?
14. Do you avoid keeping unnecessary records?
15. Do you make time for special creative work?
16. Do you do all you can to avoid creating rush jobs?
17. Are there appropriate mechanical aids?
18. Is there sufficient equipment—no avoidable time loss during sharing and waiting?
19. Is the equipment accessible and properly maintained?
20. Do you ensure that the layout does not result in unnecessary movement?
21. Are there excessive personal conversations and interruptions?
22. Are the staff seated in the best position in relation to each other and the supervisor?
23. Do you periodically (every 6 months?) review your departmental layout showing positions of staff, records and equipment?

Questions	✕ ✓	*Notes*
24. Have you a good follow-up system?		
25. Do you keep a log book recording the department's activities and messages in and out?		
26. *Backlog*		
(a) Are you sure the backlog is not resulting in poor service to the public?		
(b) Are you sure it is not causing additional work, reminders, issue of additional documents, difficulty in finding papers, failure to put through accounting entries or to advise account amendments in time?		
(c) Do you check whether the arrears are spread generally or confined to one or a few individuals?		
(d) Do you find out how the backlog arose— staff shortages or changes, uneven allocation of work, lack of instruction or help?		
(e) Do you examine what can be done about it—remove it entirely from the individual, stop allocating further work, redistribute, provide assistance, or have a team blitz?		
(f) Do you plan longer-term remedies to prevent a recurrence?		
(g) Do you frequently examine the records of work outstanding?		

Question

1. Describe how you would set about planning a major painting and decorating project in a medium sized factory which has a two-week summer shut down.

18. *Using initiative when work is delegated to you*

As a supervisor you have to receive delegated work and think through the problems which arise in the course of your duties. Sometimes the issues involved are not ones on which you are authorized to act, but your boss will want your recommendations.

The concept of *completed staffwork* is useful here. This is the study of a problem and the presentation of a solution by a supervisor to his manager in such a way that all that remains to be done by the manager is to give a decision. The more difficult a problem is, the more tendency there is to refer it to the manager in a piecemeal fashion.

It is your job to work out the details, consulting other supervisors and specialists such as personnel, training, industrial engineering staff and, if permissible, appropriate sources of information outside of the company.

The impulse which sometimes comes to the supervisor to ask his manager what action to take happens more often when the issue is difficult. It is sometimes accompanied by a feeling of frustration, because it is so easy to ask the manager what to do and it appears easy for him to answer. You will be more helpful if you can advise him what you think he should do rather than ask him what move you should make. It will alleviate his work load if you can consider alternative solutions and possible courses of action and select what you consider to be the best solution. He needs answers not questions.

Do not worry your boss with long explanations and memos. Writing a memo to him is less useful than writing a memo for him to send to someone else. Your views should be placed before him in finished form so that he can make his decision simply by signing his name. If he wants comment or explanation he will ask for it. The concept of completed staffwork does not preclude a rough draft, but this must not consist of half-baked ideas, used as an excuse for shifting the burden to the manager.

This way of operating may result in more work for the supervisor, but it gives the manager more freedom by shielding him from unnecessary detail. Moreover the supervisor who has a real idea to sell is more likely to achieve its acceptance.

When you have finished your completed staffwork the final test is this:

If you were the manager would you be willing to sign for the solution you have recommended, and stake your professional reputation on it?
If not, it's 'back to the drawing board'.

If you adopt this way of working, discussion of the assignment with a manager has a proper place when establishing guidelines and method of approach. This is particularly advisable in lengthy investigations where, if the terms of reference were not agreed with the manager initially, time could be wasted. Sometimes a progress report is desirable, and you should find out whether your boss needs one.

The overriding principle is that you should not dodge the responsibility for thinking a problem through in all its aspects.

Next time you hit a snag with a major project, but have some good ideas about solving it; or you have an idea for improving efficiency, cutting costs or reducing accidents; or your boss has asked you to look into a problem and come up with some recommendations—this could be your cue for some completed staffwork.

If you are in doubt about how your boss would take to this way of working, why not let him read this chapter and say if it fits in with his views?

Preventive and contingency plans

The legend of the sword of Damocles tells how a sword was suspended by a hair over the Greek hero's head. At any time the hair might break. Have you ever had that feeling? Preventive and contingency plans are arrangements which will either remove the threat (why did he have to just stand there?) or minimize the consequences if the threat should materialize (safety helmet). Good maintenance *prevents* a car breaking down, and a tool kit in the boot is useful for contingency purposes.

You not only keep above a minimum stock level of frequently used parts, but you have the telephone number of a supplier who would send them on the panic wagon if the need arose. Always foresee snags and take precautions, besides earning the reputation of having a card or two up your sleeve if the worst comes to the worst.

Creative thinking

Creative thinking is the process of generating ideas, whether these are needed in order to overcome snags or to break new ground. One of the best books I have ever read on this subject is *Lateral Thinking for Management* by Edward de Bono (McGraw-Hill). He points out that we tend to get into a mental rut and think along tramlines instead of jumping out (laterally) and exploring a wider range of ideas. His techniques for doing this are extremely effective and I can only recommend that you obtain the book and try them for yourself. Here are a number of thought-provoking questions which you might ask next time you are faced with a difficult problem and you are stumped for ideas. The following list has often helped supervisors and managers out of a difficult spot by suggesting a new approach.

Decision making

Notes for generating alternative courses of action
  1. Have I done this sort of thing before? How?
  2. Could I do this in some other way?
  3. How did other people tackle it?

4. What kind of people am I dealing with?
5. How can this situation be changed to fit us?
6. How can we adapt to fit this situation?
7. How about using more?
>>>>>>>>>>>>>>>>>>>>>>all of it?
>>>>>>>>>>>>>>>>>>>>>>one?
>>>>>>>>>>>>>>>>>>>>>>two?
>>>>>>>>>>>>>>>>>>>>>>several?
>>>>>>>>>>>>>>>>>>>>>>less than we have done?
>>>>>>>>>>>>>>>>>>>>>>only a portion?
8. How about using something else?
>>>>>>>>>>>>>>>>>>>>>>older?
>>>>>>>>>>>>>>>>>>>>>>newer?
>>>>>>>>>>>>>>>>>>>>>>more expensive?
>>>>>>>>>>>>>>>>>>>>>>cheaper?
9. How near?
10. How far?
11. In what direction?
12. Could I do this in combination?
>>>>>>>>>>>>>>>>>>>>>>with whom?
>>>>>>>>>>>>>>>>>>>>>>with what?
13. What about doing the opposite?
14. What would happen if I did nothing?
15. What specialist advice is available within the organization?
16. What external bodies could give advice?
17. What do subordinates, colleagues, superiors, suggest?
18. Does company policy suggest any particular approach?
19. Do the usual constraints really apply in this case?

Fig. 18.1. Checklist on initiative

Questions	✕ ✓	Notes
1. Do you anticipate bottlenecks and take steps to eliminate them?		
2. Do you keep abreast of changes in methods, materials, and machinery, and are you able to discuss them with your superior?		
3. Have you checked that there are no long-standing anomalies in your department? If there are, have you a plan for eliminating them?		
4. Do you take advantage of any useful training which is available?		
5. Do you acknowledge scope for improvement in your department and take steps to achieve it?		
6. Do you think out alternative solutions to put to your superior when you do not yourself have the authority to take action on the problem?		
7. Do you ensure that action taken is not wasted through lack of follow-up?		
8. Can you be relied upon to see problems through within the scope of your job, regardless of most obstacles?		

NB. Using initiative does not mean acting without authority.

Question

1. What is meant by completed staffwork and how is it likely to benefit
   (a) the boss,
   (b) the employee who does it?

19. *Management tool subjects*

The tools of management are systematic or scientific techniques for solving business problems. You should acquire some knowledge of these so that you can follow up and learn more about any technique which could help your company. Perhaps some of these specialized fields could open up new career opportunities for you or members of your staff. A year or two in, say, work study can be a useful springboard to a more senior line management job. The following are some of the terms you may come across in this connection.

Activity sampling   The process of making systematic periodic checks on what an employee or machine is doing in order to build up a picture of how the time is spent. This could reveal, for example, that there was far too much time wasted in travelling, and thus pinpoint the need for a better layout.

Brainstorming   Calling together a group of people who could contribute to the solution of a problem and letting them spark off ideas. Certain rules are followed to sustain the creativity of their thinking—for example, at the freewheeling stage no one is allowed to dismiss an idea as nonsense. All ideas are evaluated rationally when the group has finished its flights of fancy.

Creative Thinking and Brainstorming, J. G. Rawlinson, BIM.

Computers   Computers are simply rapid calculating machines.

Systems analysis: the process of looking at a problem requiring rapid calculations and deciding whether the computer can solve it and in what way.

Programming: the job of applying the specification laid down by the systems analyst, and translating the pieces of information into data which the computer can handle.

Operating: the process of putting the information into the computer or getting it out. Computer operators produce punched cards or paper tapes from which the information is transferred onto computer tapes or discs.

Control ratios   Simple ratios such as per cent rejects, accidents per 1000 man hours, cost per mile, man hours lost/man hours worked, machine running time/maintenance time, are an aid in keeping control of the work of the department. They enable the company as a whole to keep track of the trends in its operations, and to compare its performance with other organizations.

Successful Managerial Control by Ratio Analysis, Spencer A. Tucker, McGraw-Hill.

Corporate planning   A systematic approach to the task of deciding the company's long-term objectives and making sure that everybody acts in accordance with the master plan.

Corporate Strategy, H. I. Ansoff, McGraw-Hill.
Corporate Planning, John Argenti, Allen & Unwin.

Cost benefit analysis   This technique helps you to express in money terms the usefulness of different kinds of expenditure when there is no direct financial return, for example: Would it be better to have new cycle racks or an extension to the works canteen?

Critical path   See page 203.
Critical Path Planning, K. M. Smith, Management Publications Ltd.

Cybernetics   The science of control. A very simple example of a cybernetic system is a thermostat; the temperature reaches a certain point and the thermostat cuts off the heater. The same principles are being developed in order to help solve management problems which require action when certain conditions occur.

Decision trees These are procedure diagrams showing alternative courses of action you should take according to circumstances, e.g., has the employee brought a sick note from his doctor on returning to work? YES—he can start work. NO—he must report to the nurse. A more complicated decision tree looks like a diagram of branches, hence the name given to this technique.

Discounted cash flow If you invest in a useful piece of equipment or plant you have to raise the money and probably pay in instalments. At a certain stage the cash begins to come in. The discounted cash flow technique helps you to phase income and expenditure to the company's advantage.

Appraisal of Investment Projects, D.C.F., A. M. Alfred and J. B. Evans, Chapman & Hall.

Ergonomics The study of the positioning of the employee in relation to his desk, bench, seat, pedals, levers, etc., in order to suggest improvements in design or layout which will achieve maximum operator efficiency and comfort.

Gantt charts A Gantt chart represents in the shape of a rectangle the available working hours for a machine in a week or month. You plot the work out in the available hours, thus showing available spare capacity. The effects of delays can easily be assessed and the manufacturing programme adjusted accordingly.

Fig. 19.1. Simplified Gantt chart

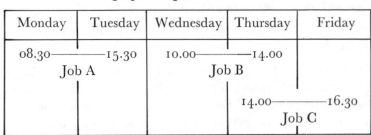

Monday	Tuesday	Wednesday	Thursday	Friday
08.30————15.30 Job A		10.00————14.00 Job B		
			14.00————16.30 Job C	

Job evaluation   A systematic way of assessing the value of a job in comparison with another, so that fair differentials can be established within the company.

Job Evaluation, T. T. Rawlinson, Business Books Ltd.

Lateral thinking   See chapter 18.

Lateral Thinking for Management, E. de Bono, McGraw-Hill.

Market research   The process of finding out what the potential customer wants before you spend too much on research, development, and manufacture. It also enables a company to improve existing products.

Merit rating   A systematic way of assessing what salary a particular employee merits. You usually establish by job evaluation a possible maximum and minimum for his position, and on an assessment of his merit you grade his salary within that bracket.

Method study   See **Work study**.

Operational research   This is a wide field covering a number of techniques, mostly mathematical, which apply the scientific method to management decision making. The applications are practically limitless, ranging from stock control to space exploration.

Operational Research, M. S. Markover and F. Williamson,
   Teach Yourself Books—EUP.

   The techniques include the following

Linear programming: the application of mathematics to problems when you must make the best use of limited resources, such as assigning vehicles to collection and delivery schedules.

Queue theory: the use of calculations to help you decide how many service points are needed (e.g., for queues at a counter) and what the business loss will be if you cut down on attendants.

Replacement theory: is it better to change the light bulbs in the factory individually when they fail, or change them all at regular periods? How long should these periods be? Replacement theory helps you to work out this kind of maintenance problem.

Simulation (models) : if you only drive a thousand miles a year the cost per mile is obviously greater than if your car does ten times that mileage. A model for this situation would be a graph which would enable you to read off the cost per mile for a given mileage. You could also have a model for the cost of domestic gas on a two part tariff. Simulation, or the use of models, means producing a theoretical picture in graphical or numerical form which will tell you what will be the cost or the effect if you make any changes.

Organization and methods   This is the study of organization structure and the administrative procedures and methods employed. What work study does for the manual side of the business, O & M does for the clerical and administrative side.

Handbook of O & M Analysis, W. A. R. Webster,
    Business Books Ltd.

The Practice of O & M, HMSO, 1965.

Process charts   These are diagrams which give you a simplified picture of a process. Symbols representing such activities as operation, inspection, transportation, delay and storage are used. Process charts are an aid to job simplification because you can challenge whether each activity shown on the diagram is really necessary.

Statistical quality control   By analysing records and samples you can statistically predict with some accuracy how frequently a production fault will occur. You will want 'zero defects' on an aircraft, but the occasional slightly defective mail bag, for example, is less critical. Statistical quality control helps you to see whether you are achieving the required standard.

A Practical Approach to Quality Control, R. H. Caplen,
    Business Books Ltd.

String diagrams A string diagram is a plan of a workplace showing the locations where different parts of the process are carried out. A pin is located at each operation point on the plan or drawing board, and a piece of string linking up the pins shows the distance travelled. By modifying the layout you can shorten this. The technique is one of the tools used in work study.

Synthetic time standards or PMTS (Predetermined Motion Time Study) In work measurement you need to find out how long each job should take. 'Synthetic' times for activities such as: *stretch out hand, grasp screwdriver*, are listed in a manual and by adding them up you can find out how long it should take to do the total job.

Methods Time Measurement, H. B. Maynard, McGraw-Hill.

Value analysis See chapter 15.

Value Analysis, W. L. Gage, McGraw-Hill.

Variety reduction Many companies carry too many lines when most of their profit comes from just a few. Variety reduction cuts out the dead wood. When Henry Ford said 'You can have any colour car you like as long as it is black', he was thinking along similar lines.

'Variety Reduction', British Productivity Council.

Work study There are two main divisions of work study:

Fig. 19.2

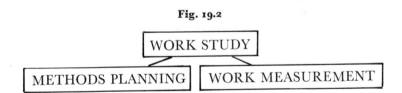

Methods planning employs a number of techniques for finding the best way of doing the job. Work measurement, which is usually carried out after methods planning improvements have been introduced, helps you to find out how long the job should take, thus providing a basis for production planning, and perhaps incentives.

Work Study, R. M. Currie, CBE, Sir Isaac Pitman & Sons Ltd.

20. *Employee appraisals*

During the course of your day's work you naturally compliment people on doing a good job or tactfully put them on the right lines when they have made mistakes. This on-the-spot guidance keeps the work ticking over properly, but does not always let the employee know where he stands.

It would be quite a shock to many people if they knew what their boss thought of them. Assuming that no news is good news, they carry on in their usual routine way until perhaps they see somebody else achieve a coveted promotion or be singled out for a special job, and then the truth strikes home hard. Often it is too late to do anything about it, so the employee becomes bitter and antagonistic, or swears never to put himself out again, doing only just enough to get by.

It is a good idea to have a regular six-monthly or yearly chat with each member of the team, standing back a bit from the day-to-day job and reviewing his overall progress. This gives you the following benefits:

1. You acknowledge his successes, and he will be motivated to try harder.
2. You both identify problem areas (such as bad tools, shortages, backlogs, scrap work) and can jointly plan ways of solving these difficulties.
3. You both identify his training needs and can plan how to arrange the necessary tuition or help him to help himself with private study or practice.
4. You discuss his future and can go some way towards reconciling his ambitions with his potential and the opportunities available. If these cannot be reconciled, at least you know you have the seeds of a problem there.

Reconciling his ambitions with his potential

5. You help him to sort out the priorities within his job, so that he will concentrate his efforts where they are most needed.

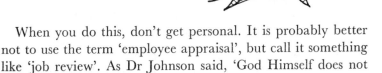

THE EMPLOYEE'S NEEDS

1. TELL ME WHAT YOU EXPECT FROM ME
   - (a) how much work
   - (b) to what quality standard
   - (c) how economically
   - (d) how quickly, etc.

2. GIVE ME WHAT IS NEEDED TO DO THE JOB
   - tools
   - training
   - materials
   - conditions
   - information
   - the right atmosphere

3. LET ME KNOW HOW I AM DOING AND HOW TO DO BETTER
   Let me continually be able to read my score on 1(a). (b). (c). (d) etc. Give me the facts and figures
   Tell me how I'm doing when you see me do something good— or when I have dropped a clanger and don't know it.
   Discuss with me once in a while where I stand in my job and what my prospects are.

4. TRY TO SEE THAT I AM FAIRLY PAID
   Recommend to the powers that be that I shall get paid according to my worth— and if they say "No", don't too easily give up asking

When you do this, don't get personal. It is probably better not to use the term 'employee appraisal', but call it something like 'job review'. As Dr Johnson said, 'God Himself does not propose to judge a man until the end of his days.' Concentrate on talking about his performance, not his character. It is damaging to destroy a person's self esteem by criticizing short-comings over which he has no control, but you can criticize the score without humiliating the player. The key to successful staff appraisal is to bear in mind the employee's needs, as shown on the Scroll on page 223.

How do you decide what you expect from an employee?

Sometimes this is laid down for you, or determined by work study, or perhaps there is a well established standard which everybody accepts in your industry. Beware though, that you are not stuck with an outdated and easily achieved level of performance which may have been satisfactory ten years ago under different circumstances. One weaving department which I visited had been content with a loom efficiency of 50 per cent until the new management team set the 'impossible' target of 70 per cent. Now they have surpassed 72 per cent.

If there are no existing standards worth speaking of, decide, in the light of your boss's objectives, what you should aim for. Then discuss with your team, individually or as a group, how these goals can be achieved. Tell them what you want from each of them, and ask them what they need from you in order to score. If you set the right atmosphere they will admire you for this. I once firmly believed that no training officer should attempt to spend more than one week in four conducting courses until somebody showed me otherwise, and then I enjoyed the new tempo. Keep a close watch on them, though, for signs of strain.

Wherever possible, you should try to *measure* performance so that there is a figure, percentage, or ratio to go by. This makes it easier for people to see what they are doing. Instead of just asking people to work faster, improve quality, reduce costs, or prevent accidents—you set a production quota, reject rate, cost per unit, or target for days worked without a lost time accident.

Sometimes you cannot exactly measure a particular standard

of performance, such as the skill of a welfare officer, for example, but do not let this fact put you off. The main requirement of a standard is that it should mean the same thing to the two or three people who are using it. While it is better to have facts rather than opinions, if a boss and his subordinate looking at an aspect of the work ask themselves 'How do we tell when it is being well done?' and after discussion arrive at a definition which is meaningful to both of them, then that definition is a valid standard. In making some of the most important business decisions ('Will it sell?' 'Will he fit into the job?' 'Should we trust them?') judgement as well as measurement must be used. Any standard which helps you to distinguish failure from success is better than none at all.

Valid measurements

Any measurements used must be accepted as valid by those using them. For example, if the frequency of accidents is used as a measurement of a supervisor's effectiveness in training his staff, he must believe that this is a valid and fair yardstick.

Here are some examples of the sort of yardsticks you could use:

Percentages, e.g., not more than X per cent machine down time.

Frequency of occurrence, e.g., staff appraisals are done every six months or jobs re-evaluated at least once every year.

Averages, e.g., production averages X thousand per week.

Time limits, e.g., departmental budgets are ready before 1 April.

Absolute prohibition, e.g., no employee starts work without receiving a lecture on safety.

Reference to external standards (legislation, etc.), e.g., the quality of training is up to Industrial Training Board standards.

Should we measure only outputs?

It is obviously preferable to use as a standard the end *result*, or output of the job. For example, in assessing a motorist's performance, you would look at his record of accidents and motoring convictions. But a Ministry of Transport learner driver examiner has to base his judgements largely on 'inputs'. 'Does the candidate know his Highway Code?', and so on.

If you cannot define any good output standards, do not be reluctant to define the input, i.e., a prescribed way of working known to give effective results. For example, you might specify as one of the standards of effective recruitment that aptitude tests are used.

Why write down standards?

Standards are of greater value if they are recorded. The piece of paper must not be seen as an end in itself but used as a living instrument in the process of supervision.

What other sources of standards exist?

The Centre for Inter-firm Comparisons of the British Institute of Management acts as a focal point for supervisory and managerial standards, and so do many of the trade and professional associations, the latter often being extremely specific and detailed in non-managerial areas as well.

When you have agreed what you want your team to do, and how you will be able to tell when they are on target, you must listen to what your staff say they want from you in order to do what is expected of them. This takes care of point 2 on the Scroll.

Point 3 is partly achieved by ensuring that he can always read his score card, by giving him guidance on a day to day basis as needed, and doing your six-monthly or yearly review.

The six-monthly or yearly job review interview

Before you ask him to discuss this with you, let him know well in advance so that he can prepare for it. You could give him the following questions to think about for a week beforehand, in order to help him collect his thoughts:

What have you accomplished during the period?
Are there any changes which you would wish to see that will

help you to accomplish more in the forthcoming year?

Do you think you have complete understanding of the requirements of your job?

Are there any aspects of the job which are vague?

Which parts of your job do you do best?

Which parts of the job are you not quite so happy about?

Do you think you have skills and aptitudes which are not fully used in your present job?

What training do you think would help you to improve your performance in your present job?

Choose the right time for the interview

Make sure he is at his best, not tired and touchy. Just prior to the job review, make the following preparations:

1. Set aside an hour.
2. Choose a suitable place Don't talk across a table or desk as this can create a barrier.
3. Ensure against interruptions by telephone or visitors.

Prepare thoroughly

Read in advance, and keep at hand:

1. His personal history sheet, file or record card.
2. A summary of the training he has received.
3. A note of any targets he has been going for during the period under review.
4. A note of his success or lack of it, in attaining these.

Consider:

1. What he has been up against (e.g., problems with work pressure, material shortages, equipment, etc.).
2. What work he has had to pull in over and above his normal work.

The interview

Use the plan shown in Fig. 20.1 for a guide.

Fig. 20.1

1. Ask him what he feels he has achieved during the year.	2. Ask him what were the main problems he felt he was up against. If you can see a problem he hasn't recognized, state it and ask for his suggestions. Tactfully contribute yours.
3. Discuss with him his year's targets.	4. Ask him what help he needs, including any training requirements.

Listen more than you talk. The chapter on selecting staff gives some advice on encouraging interviewees to speak up for themselves. By listening you can check whether he has a clear idea of the work to be done and the priorities involved. If he hasn't you can guide him towards a better understanding of these matters. The secret of encouraging a person to talk is in asking the right kind of questions.

Ask open questions. Don't ask leading questions, that is, ones which imply the answer by the way they are phrased. Leading questions always carry an assumption, such as 'I take it . . .' 'I suppose . . .' 'Presumably . . .' 'No doubt . . .' or ' . . ., doesn't it?' So unless you are 200 per cent certain you are right, avoid such remarks as : 'I suppose you've had problems with your machine?'

'No doubt the trainee held you back a bit?'

'I suppose you wouldn't mind going over to shift work?'

'Reflect'. When he makes a comment, show that you can understand what he is getting at (even though you might not agree that he is right) by putting his views back to him in your own words. If you must, you can disagree with him later, but it makes sense to encourage him to express himself fully first, so that you really understand what it is you are disagreeing with.

This is the technique mentioned in chapter 6 on grievance interviewing.

Here is an example of how the interview might work out:

BOB (*the manager*): Hullo Jack, come in and take a seat. Coffee?

JACK: Hullo Bob, thanks.

BOB: Did you have a chance to think about the questions I gave you the other day? You know, the ones about this progress report?

JACK: Yes, where shall we start?

BOB: Let's start with what you've achieved during the last six months. Is there anything you would especially single out?

JACK: I suppose it was something just to keep up production especially during February with all the power problems.

BOB (*responding to Jack's mood*): That took some doing.

JACK: You know, I think the firm should buy its own generator.

BOB (*who refrains from arguing with Jack that if there's an oil shortage it may hit supplies to private generators, which would mean £5000 worth of investment standing idle*): You feel a generator would help.

JACK: Yes, even if there was rationing we would be allowed a small emergency stock which would get us out of some of the real trouble we hit mid-February with the Thompson order. That set us back £10 000.

BOB: I'll make a note of that suggestion, Jack. Can't promise anything, but it's worth thinking about. What else would you feel was outstanding about the last six months?

JACK: Well, Bob, I think I made out pretty well during the week you were away at the European exhibition and I deputized for you.

BOB: You feel the week went pretty smoothly.

JACK: I had my worries of course.

BOB: You were bothered at times.

JACK: Yes, they asked me some tricky questions about the quality standards and I felt I would have done better if I had a better knowledge of inspection.

BOB: You would like a bit of training in that. Any particular point you need to know about?

(Jack was fairly pleased with himself about the week's deputizing. Bob, the manager, was pleased with the way he had held the fort, but knew that there were a few problems. However, he refrains from deflating Jack, but gets him to appreciate his own shortcomings, and to recognize that he needs training. The secret is in reflecting, showing *empathy*, tuning in to his mood, and letting him discover things about himself by considering the right questions.)

No surprises. There should be such good regular day-to-day and week-to-week communication between you and each member of your team that very little comes as a surprise to him during the job review. For example, if it came out in this chat that you thought the quality of his work was below average and he had been under the impression that his work was good, you would know that in future he needed more frequent guidance.

Although comments in these reviews should be more or less as anticipated, such interviews are well worth while as they permit you both to take an overall view.

View the whole year, not just recent events. A bad mistake he made last week should not distort your assessment of him over the year as a whole.

References to other employees and their work. When discussing Tom's work with him, don't compare it favourably or unfavourably with Harry's. Word always gets back to the person criticized and either way it tends to undermine relationships.

Summarize at the end. Recap on the main points, especially the action you are each going to take, and then end the chat on an encouraging note.

If you don't think he can take it, don't give it. If your knowledge of the individual and his personal circumstances and state of mind tell you that criticism of his performance will only make it worse, don't criticize. Let him do all the talking. There are times when even the best medicine can harm a patient. Commonsense must prevail over all formal systems, and if the system says you have got to appraise every employee, keep it short and sweet in cases like this.

Fig. 20.2. Checklist on appraisal interviewing

Questions	× √	Notes
1. Do you have a six-monthly talk with each of your employees about his progress at work?		
2. Do you let him know a week in advance so that he can prepare himself?		
3. Do you prepare yourself by having his records available, especially any notes about his achievements or problems?		
4. Do you plan what you are going to tell him and ask him?		
5. Do you set aside an hour for the interview?		
6. Do you organize a comfortable room with no desk to act as a barrier?		
7. Do you ensure against telephone/visitor interruptions?		
8. When you conduct this interview do you listen twice as much as you talk?		
9. During the interview do you: (a) ask open questions? (b) reflect?		
10. Do you summarize what has been discussed and recap on the points for action?		

Questions

1. Do you think job review discussions are useful? Please give your reasons.

2. What preparations should you make before the interview?

3. What do you think are the important *dos* and *don'ts* to be observed when reviewing an individual's performance?

21. *Supervision in the office*

About four million people out of a working population of 23 million in the UK are employed in offices. This figure includes those who work in the rapidly growing field of computers. Office staff may be engaged in national and local government, public utilities, clerical departments within companies, and in large office-based organizations like banks and insurance companies.

Their speed and efficiency are, of course, as vital to our economy as those whose jobs have a more tangible end product, for all the achievements in research, production and sales would be wasted without effective clerical support.

It is important to put this point across to your team in the office, and particularly to the younger members of staff, some of whom may feel that their contribution is nebulous, and that their cost is just an overhead.

Nearly all of this book is as relevant to the office supervisor or manager as to his counterpart who controls the work of manual staff. One particularly important aspect, however, which has not yet been mentioned, is liaison with the operating departments.

The need to liaise effectively

If you are the supervisor or manager of a department which provides a service to a manufacturing, servicing or construction organization it is vital to maintain effective liaison across the line to the blue-collar side. All too often there is a breakdown in communication, and sometimes even of regard between the two parts of an organization. Each considers the other to be living in a world of its own and the passage between them is referred to as 'the great divide'. One has to remember that the office is there to provide a service—whether it is accounting, computers, personnel, or administration—for the operating departments.

The communication barrier can be broken down in the following ways.

The right attitude from the top. If the manager makes it clear that he expects his staff to put themselves out to help, and shows by his attitude that he recognizes that the production worker produces everybody's bread and butter, and should be accorded due respect, then his staff will fall in line too.

Make it clear to your staff that effective interdepartmental liaison is an important facet of their job. Mention this point in annual job review interviews.

Introduce new staff to those with whom they will have to liaise. This breaks down the feeling that each category is a breed apart. Staff feel involved from the beginning.

Expect staff to know basic technical terms. For example, if the company makes lubricants, every office worker should have a reasonably good knowledge of what terms like 'viscosity' mean.

Set a good example. Make sure you circulate at works outings or company functions. Eat with some of the production supervisors and managers in the staff canteen, so that you get to know their problems. Don't stick to a small clique.

Get to know personally every new production manager and supervisor. You will find they will then cooperate with you whenever you need their help.

Don't make unreasonable demands. What looks important from a tidy administrative point of view may not be reasonable from the production man's standpoint, so don't overburden supervisors with paperwork. Make new systems easy for them.

Consult supervisors and managers about administrative changes which affect them. They will go along with these changes more readily if they can see the need for them and have been invited to comment.

Self development for the office supervisor

Chapter 5 dealt with training and self development, and most of its contents are applicable to the office, but the following areas need special attention:

Recruitment and selection of staff (chapter 3).
Interviewing (chapters 3, 6, 20).
Staff appraisal (chapter 20).
Staff training and instruction techniques (chapter 5).
Leadership and motivation (chapters 1 and 2).
Industrial relations (chapter 11).
Job evaluation, salary administration, oral and written communication.
Delegating work (chapter 12).
Planning and organizing (chapter 17).
Methods improvement (chapter 14).
Clerical work measurement.
Safety and fire prevention (chapter 10).
Problem analysis and decision making.
Conducting meetings and discussions.

In addition you need to be proficient in the following areas:

1. The *profession* with which the particular office may be connected. For example, the head of a section in the purchasing, invoice, accounts, or personnel departments has to have specialist knowledge.
2. The *procedures*, such as how a payroll is processed or which documentation is required in licensing a vehicle.
3. The *equipment* in the office, including typewriters, duplicating equipment, guillotines, etc. Some pieces of equipment such as calculating machines, typewriters and punch card machines require a high degree of manual dexterity but it is not

normally necessary for the office supervisor himself to possess this skill.

In our supervisors' discussion groups on this topic, several hundred people have suggested the following useful ideas for developing one's knowledge in these areas:

The profession

Join professional bodies.
Read up books and magazines on the subject.
Subscribe to at least one professional magazine.
Consult colleagues and superiors.
Attend evening classes.
Take correspondence courses.
Mix socially with members of the profession.
Discuss with colleagues the company procedure guides on this subject.

The procedures

Learn from the practitioners in your department.
Ask them for tuition. Never be afraid to learn from a subordinate.
Ask to be allowed to do a job according to the procedure and get somebody to check your work.
Read up the relevant company procedure guides.

The equipment

Ask the experienced operators to show you.
Attend manufacturers' courses (e.g., on litho duplicating).
Read the manufacturers' instruction manuals.

Training office staff

In offices where there are a fair number of newcomers to train in well established jobs, it is a good idea to produce a *training analysis and programme* such as the one shown in Fig. 21.1.

The *main duties* are the important jobs to be done by the person concerned, while the *tasks* are a more detailed specification of what each duty involves.

Fig. 21.1. Training analysis and programme (Position: order clerk)

Main duties	Tasks	Skills/knowledge required	Normal programme (tutor and duration)
1. Take telephone orders.	Record particulars.	Effective telephone communication.	Training dept 1 day (Standard course)
	Advise customer about delivery.	Special customers.	Supervisor 1 day
		Products.	Sales dept ½ day
		Availability.	Supervisor 1 day
		Discounts.	Stores 1 day
		Freighting or delivery method.	Shipping dept ½ day
	Process the order.	Procedure.	Section head 3 days
2. Maintain stock levels.	Maintain stock-control records.	Stock cards and codes.	Stores 2 days
	Order when necessary.	Minimum stock levels.	Supervisor ½ day
		Discounts for quality.	Section head 1 day
		Alternative suppliers.	Purchasing dept 2 days
		Alternative products.	Supervisor 1 day

The other two columns specify the knowhow needed, and the means by which it should be acquired.

Further education for office staff

Your staff without GCEs or CSEs may find it useful to study for the Certificate in Office Studies (or the Scottish Certificate in Office Studies), or, if they have the requisite number of GCE/CSE passes, the Ordinary National Certificate in Business Studies.

These courses give a broadly based education in the principles and methods of business. You can obtain particulars from your local College of Further Education. For more advanced training, the Polytechnic can advise you.

Students in Scotland can select from a range of courses in office studies which have been devised by the Scottish Council for Commercial, Administrative and Professional Education.

Ways to improve efficiency

If you have not yet attended an Organization and Methods appreciation course lasting about a week, it is important that you should do so. Your local Polytechnic or technical college probably organizes these, or your Training Board could tell you where to enrol. Much of the TWI course for office supervisors, which also covers other subjects, is devoted to methods improvement and you can find out about this training from the Department of Employment.

The right O & M appreciation course will include such subjects as:

Work simplification.
Critical analysis of existing procedures.
Devising new procedures.
The design of forms.
Records and files.
Office lay-out.
Electronic data processing (outlined).

Analysing and redistributing workloads.
Activity sampling.
The effective use of time.
Clerical work measurement.

The advantage of taking a good course is that you get involved in practical work, and in this subject it is particularly important to learn by doing. But while you are waiting to attend, the following books may help you:

A Handbook of O & M Analysis, W. A. R. Webster,
    Business Books Ltd.
Office Organisation and Methods, G. Mills and O. Standingford,
    Pitman.
Office Administration, J. C. Denyer, Macdonald & Evans Ltd.

These will give you a good background and useful ideas for immediate implementation.

Additional useful books on related subjects are:

Recruitment and Selection of Typists and Secretaries, Eva Roman and
    Derek Gould, Business Books Ltd.
Modern Commercial Knowledge, L. W. T. Stafford, Macdonald &
    Evans Ltd.

One point which all O & M staff stress repeatedly is that you must communicate with and consult your staff before, during and after a methods improvement programme.

Supervisors often have to do much of the work themselves, especially in small offices or ones in which they have most of the expert knowledge (e.g., accountants). This may mean they have little time, or simply forget, to communicate with staff.

The importance of the group

Every team, whether it consists of scaffolding erectors, mine rescue men, or office staff, has its self image. If you are a scaffolder your life depends on your workmates' reliability, cooperation, and nerve, so each man sees himself cast in that mould and is reluctant to accept a newcomer who isn't. Mine rescue men have similar qualities and in addition have to be extremely fit physically, in their twenties, and with a sense of dedication which will take them to any lengths to effect the recovery of a trapped miner. To fit in there, you have to be that kind of a person.

The office has its self image, too. People tend to take clerical jobs partly for status reasons, and you often find an element of initial coolness towards anyone who dresses, speaks, or behaves differently. It is not just 'cattiness'; the pressure to conform is strong.

You can minimize this problem if you consider future relationships when you interview applicants. It is no use taking on anyone you can get if this is going to cause restlessness and lead to resignations. If recruitment is that desperate, why not try flexible working hours? Offices often lend themselves readily to this.

Another way of counteracting this 'exclusive' attitude is to pay special care to the induction of new team members. Help them across barriers, train them, and see that at an early stage they are contributing effectively to the work of the department.

The future

Many modern trends—such as the achievement of a more uniform and generally higher level of education, the growth of unionization among white-collar employees, the raising of the status of blue-collar staff, and greater social mobility—are blurring the distinctions between the two groups of workers. If managers and supervisors act wisely this will lead to better liaison at work and ultimately enrich society as a whole.

Questions

1. What steps should you take in selecting a new member of staff?
2. How would you build teamwork in an office where little exists?
3. Suggest a cost reduction programme for an office with which you are acquainted.

4. What can you do to reduce the likelihood of accidents or fire in an office?
5. What are the benefits to be derived from delegating work, and how would a supervisor set about delegating more without loss of control?
6. How can liaison be improved between office and factory?
7. What do you consider are the main points to observe prior to and during an annual job appraisal interview with a member of staff?
8. What advice would you give a supervisor whose staff have recently joined a staff association and who now has to deal with a staff association representative?
9. Many disciplinary procedures stipulate the use of warning letters. Do these serve a useful purpose with office employees? Please give your reasons.
10. What can the office supervisor do to train himself and develop his potential
11. How would you set about devising a staff training programme in an office where the work was not being done sufficiently quickly or accurately? (Assume you have approximately 12 employees.)

Index

Accident prevention, 106–130
Accident-prone employees, 112
Accounting terms, 177–181
Activity sampling, 214
Appraisal interviewing, 221–231
Appreciation, 5
Art of listening, 74
Authority and responsibility, 89, 90, 155

Board of directors, 151
Borden UK Limited, 13
Brainstorming, 214
Breakeven, 179
Breaking jobs into steps, 60, 61
Briefing groups, 56
Budgetary control, 179

Centre for Inter-firm comparisons, 226
Certificate in Office Studies, 237
Change, introducing, 78–85
Clerical staff, 232–240
Committee assignments, 54
Communication, 98–105
Complaints, 70–77
Completed staff work, 209, 210
Computers, 214, 215
Consultation, 11
Control ratios, 215
Corah Limited, 2, 5
Corporate planning, 215
Cost accountant's role, 167
Cost accounting terms, 177–181
Cost benefit analysis, 215
Cost reduction, 166–183
Creative thinking, 211
Critical path, 203, 215
Cybernetics, 215, 216

Daily contact, 18, 56, 100, 204
D-day minus principle, 203
Decision trees, 216
Delegation, 140–149

Deputy, your, 185, 186
Dinosaur Limited, 98, 99
Direct costs:
    labour, 178
    material, 178
Discipline, 86–97
Discounted cash flow, 216
Dismissals, 95

Efficiency in offices, 237, 238
Electrical hazards, 122
Empathy, 230
Employees:
    accident-prone, 112
    individual training schedule for,
        63–65
    new, 39–46
    office, 232–240
    older, 189–192
    women, 186–189
Employment interview, 31–33
Ergonomics, 216
Example, 12

Fire hazards, 120, 121
Five rules for grievance interviews, 74,
    75
Fixed indirect overheads, 179
Forgetting, 63
Frustration, 17
Functional supervision, 154
Further education for office staff, 237

Gantt charts, 216
Grievance procedure, 76
Grievances, 70–77
Groups, 6
Guided experience, 54

Herzberg, F., 4
Human Relations, 1–24

Indirect costs:
  labour, 178
  material, 178
Individual employee training
  schedule, 63–66
Individual training needs analysis,
  63–65
Induction, 39–46
Initiative, 209–213
Injuries, 106–130
Inspection schedule, 195
Instruction, 56–63
Interviews:
  appraisal, 221–231
  disciplinary, 90–92
  employment, 31–33
  grievance, 73–76
Introducing new employees, 39–46

Job enrichment, 18–23
Job evaluation, 217
Job review interviews, 221–231
Job rotation, 54
Job specification, 25–27

Kamakazi, 8

Labour costs, 178
Lark and owl, 197–199
Lateral thinking, 217
Law, Foreword, xi
'Law of the situation', 93–94
Leadership, 1–16
Leading questions, 33
Learning plateau, 58
Liability of supervisors, 106
Liaison, 232–234
Line organization, 152, 153
Linear programming, 217

Machine downtime, 173–175
Management by exception, 147
Management by objectives, 155, 156
Managing director, 151
Managing time, 193–208
Man specification, 25–30
Market research, 217
Material costs, 178
McGregor, Douglas, 19
Measurements of performance, 224, 225
Merit rating, 217
Methods, improvement of, 161–165

Monotony, 18
Morning inspection, 18, 56, 100, 204
Motivation, 1–16

National Certificate/Diploma in
  Business Studies, 237
National Examinations Board in
  Supervisory Studies, 47
Nervous tension, 23
New employees, 39–46

Office employees, 232–240
Older employees, 189–192
Open questions, 228
Operational research, 217, 218
Organization and methods, 218
Organization, principles of, 150–160
Overhead costs, 178

Pending jobs lists, 196, 197
PERT, 203
Philips' Gloeilampenfabrieken, 18
Piecework, 2
Planning, 193–208
Predetermined motion time study
  (PMTS), 219
Process charts, 218
Productivity, 166, 168
Project work, 53

Questioning technique, the, 163–165
Questions in interviews, 228
Queue theory, 217

Recovery of overheads, 179
References, 35–37
Reflecting, 90–92, 228
Replacement theory, 217, 218
Reprimands, 90–92
Resistance to change, 78–85
Responsibility, 21, 155
Restrictive practices, 136
Retirement, 192
Rework, 176
Rush job, the, 206

Safety, 106–130
Scottish Certificate in Office Studies,
  237
Scrap, 176
Scroll, 224
Selecting staff, 25–38

Self development, 47–51
 office supervisor, 232–240
Shareholders, 151
Shop stewards, 131–139
Simulation, 218
Solvitur ambulando, 24
Span of control, 157
Special aspects of supervision, 184–192
Standard costing, 179
Standards, 224–226
Statistical quality control, 218
Stokes, Dr. John, 193
String diagrams, 219
Suggestions, 11
Supervisory training, 47–55
Suspension without pay, 94, 95
Synthetic time standards, 219

Taylor, F. W., 154
Teaching your team, 56–63
Teams, 6, 7, 8
Telephone reference, 35–37
Theory X & Y, 19
'Thermals', in interviews, 32

Tidmarsh, P. C., 7, 8
Trade Unions, 131
Training, 47–69
Training analysis for office staff, 236
Transition, school to work, 43, 44

Understudying, 53
Union representative, 131–139

Value analysis, 171–173
Variable indirect overheads, 178
Variety reduction, 219

Waiting time, 175
Waste reduction, 168–177, 181–183
Women employees, 186–189
Work measurement, 219, 220
Work structuring, 18
Work study, 219, 220

X, Theory, 19

Y, Theory, 19
Year to view organizer, 194